Me and My Friends, We No Longer Profess Any Graces

Me and My Friends, We No Longer Profess Any Graces

A PREMATURE MEMOIR

Richard Dean Rosen

The Macmillan Company, *New York, New York*
Collier-Macmillan Limited, *London*

"Memoirs of a Suburban Dilettante" first appeared in
The Harvard Advocate, Volume CIII, Number 3, December
1969. Copyright 1969 by the Editors and Trustees of
The Harvard Advocate and is reprinted by permission.

"One Entrecôte To Go, Easy on the Beárnaise: Food
as People's Art" first appeared in the March 4,
1970 edition of *The Harvard Crimson*. Copyright 1970
by *The Harvard Crimson* and is reprinted by permission.

to my wide family and James Atlas

Contents

A Note, 9

The Metaphors of a Suburban Dilettante, 13

Deedily Deedily Dee: Nonaffluent Materialism, 56

The Story of Baseball, 69

Watching the Descent from a Folding Chair, 86

Go Away Richard Brautigan, You're Not Helping
College Poetry Any, 119

Hot Sausage Links: An Allegory of American Politics, 131

One Entrecôte To Go, Easy on the Beárnaise:
Food as People's Art, 160

Wherever You Go, You End up in America:
Notes on a European Notebook, 168

A Short Cultural History of Salt Lake City, 181

The Last Chapter, 185

A Note

These pieces represent neither an arbitrary accumulation nor an irreversible order.

It is the author's vain wish that his readers will constantly make those fine connections between sentences and chapters which create the illusion of unity. Ostensibly, only two pieces relate closely to one another in terms of content. *Watching the Descent from a Folding Chair*, written a number of months after *The Metaphors of a Suburban Dilettante*, takes somewhat more detailed issue with ideas only mentioned in the latter and reflects some of the personal and political growth that took place in the intervening period.

The pronouns "I" and "We" are sometimes used almost interchangeably. In many cases, "We" is just a rhetorical device. In all cases, it should be understood that "We" does not stand for "all we young people" or even "all white radicals." More specifically, it might stand for a kind of white, middle-class child in America who can perhaps be identified in the ensuing pages. "My friends," similarly, does not refer to political and cultural acquaintances, but to my good friends who, in varying degrees, share my visions, frustrations, and inability to move certain crucial limbs.

I acknowledge all these close friends. Believing as I do in a very intricate causality, I can truthfully say that they have had a great deal to do with this piece of writing, in particular James Atlas and Paul Fry. I confess to have occasionally stolen words and ideas from some of them, but hope my victims will see my act as neither a theft nor a disservice.

This book, which concerns a period of my life whose form I can barely recognize, moves from one point in my head to another. The following pages are located in that disobedient, hardly linear dimension which connects them. It is not an apology, but an admission, that my own growth, in accordance with the age, is accelerated, unable at times to keep track of itself. I suddenly found myself attributing lines written a month before to someone else, an earlier version of the author who had to be acknowledged as a bit less perceptive, perhaps more so, at any rate different. So it is no secret that a number of people actually wrote this book, all employing my name, each one hoping to be credited with the better lines. As a result, personae are assumed then dropped, levels of understanding clash with one another, voices intrude.

Unripened cant; the remembrance of a remembered thing; an array of images rescued from the great silence; by the time you read this book, if you do, I will already be too old for what I've written, or else too young.

RDR

MATURE MEMOIR

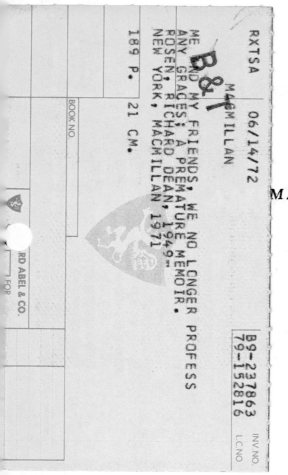

The Metaphors
of a Suburban Dilettante

The impression the Vietnamese prefer to give, and do, is of
a peaceful, viable, optimistic society. Ho Chi Minh has given,
in a speech after August 1945, a five-point recipe "For making
life optimistic": each person must 1) be good in politics,
2) be able to draw or paint, 3) know music, 4) practice some
sport, and 5) know at least one foreign language.
                                    —Susan Sontag, *Trip to Hanoi*

Naples and I must supply the world with noodles.
                                    —a patient of C. G. Jung

Being natural is simply a pose, and the most irritating pose
I know.   —Oscar Wilde

1. A Scanty History of Radical Origins

In which the author may have licentiously used but foregone
the definitions of the following terms:

Chicago	Revolution
Neighborhood Theaters	System
Older Generation	Technocracy
Politics	War Effort
Power Elite	Wild Impulse

There was one thing I was learning to accept. For so long
the recipient of the blessings of an older generation, I was now
the recipient of its uncertain wrath. After nineteen, twenty,

twenty-one years of precious nonconformity, after an adolescence pockmarked with insolence, I was going to pay for
it. Boy was I going to get it. That sense of humor and charmingly cynical attitude toward culture that my parents once
praised me for, that vision of a less turquoise, more individualized society that my teachers once rewarded me for, were
now incurring their hate. The uneasiness I had felt at high
school dances and my disapproval of Howard Johnson's did
not really disturb them; at times, they even applauded my
discontent. Sneering at politics I was only beginning to understand and hypocrisy they were certain I would learn to ration-
alize, I was considered youthfully arrogant and my grades
were considered above average.

But when my disdain for certain scabs and sores had grown
into a denunciation of a culture I saw as almost irrevocably
ill, I was suddenly dangerous and "destructive," honored, by
adults, with the same modifiers once reserved for pilose fra-
ternity brothers and hitchhiking long distances. Armed with
the same complaints as always, I was no longer loved. In fact,
I was even beaten and gassed by an older order strangely
afraid of my virility.

> Let's do the Tighten Up . . .
> To your left now, and to your right now,
> Ev'rybody can do it,
> But don't get too tight.*
>
> —Archie Bell and the Drells

On Saturday, August 24, 1968, a hip-Yip (distinctions
could not really be made from a distance) took off his shirt
in Lincoln Park, and the White Sox dropped another one to
Detroit. Four days later, we forced the system to strip itself
(since then, it has dressed itself in the most garish and out-
moded clothes available). The subliminal repression it had

always used successfully to ensure its operation was inadequate in the face of the first massive counterculture demonstration. Its "absorbent power," its "repressive tolerance," broke down. When pressed for real answers about war, racism, credibility, its only response was police force and its attendant violence. Perhaps at first, we looked upon the riots as an aberration of law enforcement, too reminiscent of our impressions of the recent Prague invasion to be wholly American, surely, this wouldn't happen again. Yet, far from being a case in which the clash of an uncommonly large crowd of dissidents and an irresistible police force created an unreasonable situation, it was a preview of a coming attraction which would make its way to neighborhood theaters all over the country, even playing short runs in towns that had never heard of flare pants.

And when the system undressed, what we saw was not a beneficent protective body. The figure, although indisputably male, had soft sagging breasts, and wherever he went, fifty cops escorted him.

For many of us, the fight first came alive in Chicago, and it was not difficult to tell the sides: we wore mostly anything, but not in any way. Some of us did not stray very far from the ordinary, but we emphasized that even Sta-press garments can be made to look disreputable. Some wandered into unknown fields of fashion, designing street wear for the occasion. Most, though, mixed their metaphors, wearing old Levis over expensive English boots or eight-dollar French sunglasses and stained T-shirts. It was all more than a style for the streets; it was a way of knowing who we were. They, of course, were mostly in shades of blue and business suits.

August 28 . . . I am down on my knees in the middle of Balbo Street. Gas is in my lungs and eyes and mouth. When I regain my vision, I am facing stopped traffic, and my blistering eyes pick out a mother perched behind the oversized wheel of a Camaro. I feel like a fool on my knees, looking up sheepishly at her. I am so accustomed to my mastery of mothers that this sudden and irritating turn of events unnerves me. I am used to their chlorophyll breath when I pass them in the aisles of stores and ask rhetorical questions about their families; I am used to gently taking their coats from them when they come to see my parents, all the while cajoling them with small stories which they believe and make them laugh; I am in the habit of concealing all the differences with a smile or some reassuring gesture in a living room, until I almost believe myself that there is no difference. But here in the street, there is nothing to hide the distances.

Yet I feel foolish only for a moment. Then, I begin to enjoy the warm vulnerability of my position. For me, kneeling in the streets is unfortunate, but it is at least colored with potential martyrdom. For the mother in the Camaro, the effect is even stronger. I am a revelation to her, an emblem, the dramatization of the relationship she has not understood all these years. That her sons, the sons of the suburbs, should find themselves gassed in the streets of the city . . . she honks her horn finally, addled by the confrontation. That it should come to this. After all the dentist appointments and the sloppy joes. Still, I notice that her heart, for all its pain, goes out to me. For just a moment, but perhaps longer, her sympathy is so total that no scoffing liberal or better judgment could steal it away from her. On my scuffed knees in the middle of Balbo, I am momentarily bathed in the glow of utter righteousness.

I am asked if everything is O.K. I ask one girl if I can help. No, she says, nothing can help. I pick myself up and run to a fountain across from the Sheraton–Blackstone. I dip my flaming head into the water. I have chosen sides.

On Saturday, the twenty-fourth, Lincoln Park was filling up like a great sinus. By early afternoon, it was stuffed with people milling about in the moist air. An old man, a newspaper wedged under his arm, walked slowly among the figures, perhaps feeling some affinity for us as he strolled aimlessly. I was to imagine these seemingly polar sympathies throughout the week. Old men minding their businesses were transformed into compatriots as disenfranchised as we. Crumpled dowagers, by virtue of their loneliness became radical sympathizers and carried handwritten manifestoes in their sequined purses. If they did appear, in fact, to be somewhat reactionary, it was because they had deliberately repressed their radical instincts. It was a ploy; by posing as antagonists, they would force us to emphasize our own radicalism greatly, hastening social change. Then, when satisfied that we had proved our sincerity, the imposters would all unmask themselves, unveil their anarchy, and the revolution would be on. Later, at Harvard, I even began to empathize with a few cops as I looked in their faces. One had a rash from shaving. In Chicago, newly indoctrinated into political radicalism, I saw the cops as menacing villains. Certainly, I saw behind them to a corrupt convention to a corrupt system, and behind Chicago, I discovered a dozen other cities that were going to fall. But to me, the cops were not just agents of a power elite, but members of it too. I was not able to dissociate them (often victims of their employer, the state) from their jobs. At Harvard, though, I was not afraid of them. In fact, I felt for them the most embarrassing thing a radical can feel: pity. Brought in by a university president to do a job, they had very little insight into the nature of the battle they were commissioned to fight. In many respects, they were being used to fight their own class interests. Before the Harvard skirmish broke out, here were hundreds of us taunting these cops as if they were somehow the core-object of our radicalism; and here were rows of cops, holding on nervously to their sticks, shuffling their feet, like a tidy, but frightened, freshman class surveying the Harvard Yard for the first time. When an injured girl shrieked to a cop, "Why are you doing this to us?" he couldn't answer. Did she really expect him to know? At one point, I had the wild impulse to rush up to a cop and ask him if he cried at his father's funeral. Anything to return to him some of the humanity he renounced every time he struck a student.

In Chicago, it had been a little different. On Wednesday,

the twenty-eighth, I met my first cop. After a long wait in
Grant Park for the negotiations with the police officials to
end and the march to the amphitheater to begin, my friends
and I walked across the bridge to Michigan Avenue for some
dinner. We walked up to the door of what turned out to be
the Sheraton–Blackstone Hotel Coffee Shoppe. Inside, I
could see black-aproned waitresses moving about tables animated with delegates and businessmen. Two large cops stood
at the door. Ignoring them with polite caution, we walked up
to the glass revolving door. One of the cops put his hand
gently on my chest, an act that, under the circumstances, was
charged with nuances neither of us were yet equipped to handle.

"Weff hoo doo thick you're going, buddy?" he said.

"Inside to eat," I explained, too afraid to use my resource
of canned sarcasm.

"Webb, beat ib!" He drummed his stick in his hand. "We
nob gonna leb you in there. You nob gonna geb in there in a
thousand years."

"Man," I said, "all we want is some dinner. We're hungry,
you know."

"Hungry, eh?" the cop said. "If you don't geb outa here,
I'm gonna personaby gib you a fiss sandwiss. What do you
thick of that?"

That's a pretty good one, I thought, but was already backing
off. He had moved fully in front of me, intent on playing the
heavy.

"You all nubbing but fabbots," he laughed. "Fabbots. We
gob places for guys like you." He jabbed the other cop in the
stomach. "Like jails, eh Tony?"

Tony looked up and smiled slowly.

In reality, of course, the Great Polarization had begun.
Dowagers with their manic lipstick were not even impartial
observers; instead they sent congratulatory letters to Daley
and Pusey, as though their daughters had just been married.

At Harvard, moderates, in their own frustrating way, supported the strike yet obfuscated the issues. Professors whose
courses endeared us turned against the politics their lectures
had helped to develop. The bland masks, thought to have
concealed more enlightened expressions, turned out to be the
faces themselves.

". . . but don't put Vaseline on *after* you've been gassed,"
a polo-shirted girl instructed marshals sitting on an embankment in Lincoln Park. "Man, that's just not gonna do any
good then. . . . Back injuries? For God's sake, don't touch
the injured man. . . . Keep a wet towel in a Baggie; you can
put it over your mouth if you get gassed." Inside the brick
house at the top of the embankment Saturday, five or six old
men played cards in the large barren anteroom. They huddled
around a dank folding card table while a fan droned over the
doorway. For years, I had noticed them playing there whenever I went to the zoo, but this summer they had to bet over
the sound of the *washoi* maneuvers, the preparations, and the
crowds. Even on the sunniest days, they were inside, their
dark rumpled sports coats well defined against the cream and
light gray wall.

Late in the afternoon, a black family and friends, who were
picnicking in the park, needed a center fielder. They asked a
white hip-Yip to join their game. He did, promptly misplaying
the first ball hit to him. For a while, it looked like the most
important thing that would happen all day.

On Sunday night, the evening of the first large-scale police
raid in the park, over three thousand milled about on the
grass, talking idly with reporters and mincing in front of
photographers. "You can't take pictures in this darkness without a flash, Howie," a newsman said.

At ten fifty, some kids raised a homemade Vietcong flag
amidst a clot of people on the edge of the park. A TV arc
light hit them instantly, and cameras began to hum. By
eleven forty-five, five thousand of us were in the streets,
angrily igniting trash cans and an occasional automobile. A

small sweep by the cops started up North Avenue and turned down Wells. We started to run away, imagining pursuers, but marshals cried quickly, "Walk slow! Walk slow!" Learning the first lesson of street occupation, I walked slowly down Wells to my brother's apartment, tuned in the circus at the amphitheater, and fell asleep.

The movement was proving, as its edges softened, that it could embrace almost anybody: high-school girls, apostate liberals, wing-tipped clerks on their lunch break. Some found that ten to fifteen minutes was all that was necessary to alter their politics. Would you take in a little bourgeois materialism here and let out a little in the shoulders?

"The pigs are disturbing my peace," a boy who wore Vitalis complained to a group on the grass in the park. "When I buy marijuana, they stop me and that's disturbing my peace, because grass is peace for me. We should tie them down and force a reefer down their throats and then they'll know what life is."

On Wednesday, the gas hit me even before I crossed Clark Street on the North Side. The tear gas which had been used the night before still hung heavily in the air, and as I stepped off the curb, my eyes began to tear and burn. I turned back. Across Clark, an elderly gentleman was beginning to walk through the invisible field of vestigial gas. As he entered it, he suddenly started to rub his eyes vigorously, glancing about him. Then a woman walking through spun around sharply as though she had been pinched on the ass. She rubbed her eyes and continued on. Wanting to get over to the park, I tried to cross once again, but was repelled and retreated to the rarer atmosphere of the curb. I sat down next to two small black kids, pulled a cold plum out of a bag of fruit I was carrying, and pressed it to my irritated eyelids. I sneezed violently. "Whatcha doin'?" one of the kids smiled. "You puttin' plums on your eyes?"

At a cocktail party Thursday afternoon in the Conrad Hilton, Senator George McGovern stood at the window overlooking Michigan Avenue. "You know," he said, "until last night I was inclined to dismiss police brutality as exaggerated. But last night, when I looked out this window, I realized the stories were true."

> As you know, I have had the reputation for not going out a great deal. My reaction to last night makes it clear that I must go out more often and be more involved . . . in what are obviously troubled times. . . . What we saw was I'm afraid a very uptight establishment literally goading people . . . hitting people who had no reason to be hit. . . . Last night, I saw so-called Law and Order, without a consideration for justice or democracy. That doesn't separate us very far from totalitarian society.   —Hugh M. Hefner

O.K. What we learned at Harvard is that it can happen and might happen anywhere—at a university, on your favorite street, at weddings and grand openings, at Earl Scheib's or in bed at night. Aside from the Great Discoveries we made about our school and its complicity, not only with the war effort, but with the American way of somehow destroying all the good things we stand for, we discovered that nothing is really safe. Except maybe the liturgies and pleonasms—theirs and ours. This page, in fact, is my clean excuse for not being where I should at the moment. At Chicago, we were attending a demonstration; it was their turf. But at Harvard it was like watching murder take place in your own home.

> ". . . to your left and to your right. . . ."

In October, 1969, the Vietnam Moratorium came and went in Boston, under blue skies sprinkled with disappointing speeches. Despite its dimensions, it appeared to be devoid of crucial political power. Whereas before we had been cutting niches in the left and right sides, the top and bottom of American politics, we had now momentarily convened in the soft center. But (protracted sigh), recent movies and a heartwarming divisiveness, among other things, substantiated our

claim to a viable counterculture. SDS may die, but Jack
Kerouac lives on. He can do it. We can do it. You can do it.
She can do it. Just don't you get too tight.

Impressed at the beginning with our new identity, we clung
to a collective image which was, in fact, not entirely ours. The
mass media, in keeping with their inclination to dichotomize,
to exacerbate whatever divisions did exist, offered us descrip-
tions which pop-sociologized us, drew a convenient line between us and the rest of the world. Their epithets oversimpli-
fied our motives and abstracted our forms. They made us into
a merchandisable cult whose selling power diminished us. We
fell at first for their mechanistic categories and said to ourselves when we passed someone with long hair, "Oh, he must
be a radical too!"

When the press finally began to make distinctions, they
concerned themselves only with the most obvious points at
which radicals diverged. SDS was suddenly found to contain
factions that were as much at odds with each other as SDS
was supposed to be with the rest of America. There was talk
of cultural revolution and cultural radicals. We began to
make gross distinctions. Some had committed themselves to
a grim revolution, or at least its possibility. Some wandered
off to the countryside to form communities which exemplified
their radical, though often apolitical, aspirations. Many of us,
caught embarrassingly in the middle, were reluctant to leave
our schools and homes to redesign our lives elsewhere, but
afraid to incinerate the cities in which we had chosen to stay.
So there were those politicos whose target was an almost
unapproachable political spectre; they could be found in occupied buildings, and on probation. Then there were those
cultural radicals whose targets were the imbecilities of our
culture, not WASP culture or upper middle-class culture or
any of those sectors that even *Time* and *Life* had succeeded
in making feel self-conscious, but the qualitative crises in
American culture as a whole; they could be found in outland-

ish postures, exposing their peculiar politics on street corners, imagining their own lives to be the most effective affront of all.

We made notations on the differences between the cultural radicals, that amorphous group of aesthetic idealogues, and the politicos:

Cultural radicalism was personalized, an individual statement; political radicalism required broad and burly rhetoric, and was still strongly attached to linear thought and linear morality. In this way, political radicalism was defined by its dogma; cultural radicalism was redefined by each new culturally radical act.

Cultural radicals eschewed political rhetoric as a way of life, although they supported the principles of liberation and equality behind the cant. They also avoided close association with political groups on a permanent basis, although they allied with them during demonstrations and strikes for political leverage.

Cultural radicalism was not a power play like political revolution. For this reason, cultural radicalism was neither as expedient a cure nor as prone to failure. Cultural radicalism was exempt from the rules of politics without making final, political victories inconceivable.

Political radicalism was a reaction to politics. Cultural radicalism alluded to the ways in which many had learned that political radicalism was not just a reaction to politics but also a reaction to a cultural past, to a present culture, to Chevrolets, the game of Risk, and English 143.

We saw that the political radical's devotion to concrete changes within and without the existing political structure required a much more serious and earnestly manipulative temperament; during the occupation of an administration building, for instance, failure to conform to some devised order would result in chaos, even among radicals. Any situation, it seemed, which involved more than two people was tinged with despotism.

The political radicals tended to see the objects of their critique as at least theoretically replaceable. That is, politicians and their politics are all tangible elements which may be substituted for, with luck, through the system or, with fortitude, despite it. But political radicals often found that what they thought could be replaced could only at best be adulterated, a disappointment which drove them to greater and greater nihilisms. The cultural radicals, however, saw the ignorance of this country's people so intractable, the perversions of human motives so irremedial, that early promises of total political revolution in America, considering the economic comforts of the middle class, sounded vain. Cultural radicals turned to a kind of elitism and their strategies, absurdist and multi-sensual, were not always designed to be understood by the public, the lifelings.

Because of the cultural radicals' obvious concern for lifestyle and embellishment, the politicos charged them with being "evolutionary." There was a reason for this antagonism, however, that went beyond the difference in intensity between the two radicalisms: to be fully effective, political radicals had to be in a political context. They had to retire to a sort of battlefield, be it street confrontation, occupying buildings, or simply rhetorical debate. Cultural radicals, to be effective, needed only to bring their cultural attitude to bear on whatever situation was at hand. Whereas a cultural radical was able to express his views in an airport, the political radical would feel impotent, in need of too many props. The politicos frowned. What seemed to them to be a facile revolution of the cultural radicals was simply the enactment of the cultural radicals' equally sincere, but less explosive, strategies.

The cultural radical's means could be identical with his ends; if he decided to hold a square dance in an intersection during rush hour, that dance would be its own objective. He did not need concrete, political affirmation of its success. The cultural radical's act had intrinsic value; the political radical needed palpable proof that his had "worked."

The visually-oriented political radical had to see that his actions succeeded, but the cultural radical, usually the tribal, more audile-tactile child, discovered success merely in his ability to become involved and to involve others.

The political radical needed more proof because he competed with the government, and the most points win. As political radicals learned the rigors of competition, they learned something else; they began to acquire the colors of the species that already governed. It was self-deception to think anyone was outside the system. We did not yet play by our own rules—we only violated theirs. The attitudes some began to take on: peremptoriness, an almost totalitarian enthusiasm for their own goals, a certain expression around the mouth that quivered, between a smile and a sneer.

Finally we began to see that political and cultural radicalism were not mutually exclusive activities, but were similar vectors in a movement. And however the cultural radical distinguished himself from the political radical, the difference could be attributed to temperament and sensibility more than to a major ideological quibble. Why one radical was this and another that had more to do with the variables of family background, whether he had watched TV or read books as a child, than with chosen political views. Categories blurred; definitions served up by the media lost their validity in a week. Even the gap, the initial distinction between cultural and political radicals, was closing. We had to make finer distinctions, draw lines thinly between individuals, not groups. We became satisfied that everything "worked" in its own way. We no longer sought to accommodate the imagination of the press, but tried instead to make radicalism a way of life.

Regardless of delicate distinctions, there seemed to be a growing and common understanding about America's insanity. The sickness of the government, its politics, and its wars, only suggested a greater pathology more difficult to locate. The problem lay in the culture, resided in the inconspicuous.

Hannah Arendt argued in her essay "The Crisis in Culture"

(*Between Past and Future*) that culture survives from generation to generation, that the imperishable artifacts that wind their way across the centuries constitute culture. She even spoke of ". . . leisure time, that is, time to be devoted to culture . . ." But we listened instead to Antonin Artaud (*The Theatre and Its Double*): "This idea of a detached art, of poetry as a charm which exists only to distract our leisure, is a decadent idea and unmistakable symptom of our power to castrate . . . Once and for all, enough of this closed, egoistic, and personal art." We did not see culture as the fruits of leisure time alone, nor simply the body of objects that civilization had carefully collected to put into museums and books. Culture was not simply the refined effort, the educated piece of art.

Weren't the elements that survived, as Arendt put it, something less, merely the technological and artistic immortalities we mistook for the way we live? If we thought of culture only as that which immutably survived, it became impervious to all judgements but an artistic or technological one; the question of quality is mostly concealed. We wanted to say, instead, that culture *is*, that it is the vulnerable sum of ways we have lived and are living. If we said culture survived, we were likely to see the present only as an inviolable step in a continuum. But if we said that culture is and that we are a part of it, that it is everything that society is and produces, good and bad, perishable and immortal, home-grown and fresh-frozen, that it is both the object and its context, the cook and the casserole, culture then became susceptible to the critique of its contemporaries.

Malcolm Cowley in *Exile's Return* recalled his generation's inability to make a similar realization:

> In college we never grasped the idea that culture was the outgrowth of a situation—that an artisan knowing his tools and having the feel of his materials might be a cultured man;

that a farmer among his animals and his fields, stopping his
plow . . . might have culture without even reading a newspaper. Essentially, we were taught to regard culture as a
veneer, a badge of class distinction.

We knew that we were estranged from our politicians. The
fact that this power elite, attuned only to their own voices,
should so casually refuse to listen to the people seemed to us
a horrible violation of the Arnoldian idea of criticism that
would always "create a new current of true and fresh ideas."
We sighted political revolution at the end of this kind of hu-
manism. But there was no contact between constituents and
representatives. It was as if we were governed by an unimagi-
nable circus performing just beyond our reach. Offices were
vacated periodically, but we regarded all newcomers as only
the slightest modifications of a grim theme. They touched
history only in the sense that they were totally subservient to
it. Events became unmanageable to them; they disclaimed responsibility for conditions they had nurtured. And we were
stuck with the same war year after year like a musical which,
although it bombed in New Haven, persisted in playing to an
empty house. Really, none of us were watching, none of us
would ever play a part.

We were alienated from the government, but we turned on
the culture, which we acknowledged as the real antagonist.
We defined culture as a society's ways of life and politics was
just one of those ways. Politics, like social and religious life,
operated within a larger cultural context and assumed its character from the way we eat our breakfast, greet people on the
street, and handle our personal budgets. We saw our culture
as a disease, a set of reprehensible ways of life, and politics was
just one of the symptoms. To subvert the government, we had
to subvert the culture. Accordingly, "up against the wall" was
not simply a political threat, but a cultural warning, given to
ourselves as well as others.

2. The Neighborhood

On Saturday nights, the last train on the way from Racine to Chicago passes through town at 12:17. Lying in bed at night as a boy with no particular fondness for trains (although I had already recognized the universal and literary message of their passing), I still listened as it sped by, three blocks from my window, its hoarseness coming from everywhere at once, surrounding the house, its sound taking no direction, just a long and resonant shape in the black air. The noise came slowly, almost imperceptibly, finally overtaking me with a rasp behind which the rhythm of the wheels pumped, gasping for air. The sound settled in the neighborhood for a moment, even as the train moved on; the sound hung about the house for a moment and then caught up with the train and was carried into the distance.

The station is one of the few wood originals that haven't been replaced by square brick and cinderblock houses; its quaintness, before a winter sunset, is depicted in oils in the town library. The long dim cars have not survived. Years ago they were replaced by green and yellow double-decker models with imitation leather seats and large double doors on either side at the center of the cars. So it is not a freight train with oily black cars and flats that passes at night but an elegant succession of green and yellow cars. And it is not cattle or coal or carefully packed boxes of kitchen appliances that go by, but a few boys from Waukegan and sailors from the fort and housekeepers who come up to dust credenzas and polish silver during the day or the week in lakeside homes and are driven to the station at night to take the train back to the city.

Though these things are well known, it is not impossible to imagine in bed something quite different. In the dark, the train is displaced, moving without locale, a sound whose only destination is its extinction a mile out of the station. And whether the train is carrying commuters or whether it carries

furniture or hens, it is really nothing but a disembodied sensation, a desolate and provocative stirring in your sleep, a slight
adjustment in the night.

The same train passes at 7:37, 8:37, and 9:37, but it is not
the same as when it passes at 12:17. The street that leads from
the house to the station is entirely familiar to me during the
day. I am intimate with the houses on one side and the school-
yard on the other to the point of boredom. I know what the
yards are like. I am so familiar with the sensation of approaching the intersection in front of the one block of stores in the
car that the sensation has become like an object to me; the
whole idea of crossing that spot where the three streets meet,
of looking for cars, and finally accelerating past the hardware
store has been transformed into a very common article, like a
scotch tape dispenser. The idea of opening the glass door at
the drugstore and going in to buy a tube of Palmolive Brush-
less has been worn thin. As has the idea of going into their
small, specially humidified room where the cigars are kept.
And going to Augie the shoe repairman for Neolite soles is
an act I have performed too many times. Sometimes I think
that there is nothing about the street that leads from the
house to the station that I don't already know. But at night,
when I walk down to the drugstore to mail a letter, when the
darkness isolates every object, when the facades of the houses
are shaded and incomplete, when the night has reduced the
cosmos of the block to its embarrassing, individual parts, when
the sparse streetlights pluck certain areas from darkness but
leave others to pile up in one dimension, it is a street I don't
recognize. The electric clock in the barbershop, presiding over
the vacant chairs and the chrome instruments lined up on the
counter, is the most unfamiliar object I have ever known; it
is not a clock so much as an apparition, a curiosity that I have
invented. The warming hut at the school, barely visible from
the street, looks like a small cottage on a moor, and the school
itself, gathering its immense gabled shapes in the dimness, is
not the grammar school I went to, but someone else's, the

image of the school attended by Pierre Joseph Proudhon, by someone whose biography I have just read.

And when I passed my own town one night on my way to Chicago from Milwaukee and I looked briefly down the street at the quiet row of stores, I was not even aware that it was my town, but thought instead that it was just one of those villages, those anonymous agitations of the landscape you are used to passing in trains late at night on your way to Chicago or Tulsa.

3. The Affluence of Choice

When I was in third grade, I took drum lessons from Mr. Gandy. Mr. Gandy was a large man with a dark cobalt beard, the kind of figure you find lounging in the saloon in westerns. I was a small boy, the kind of eight-year-old who wore intricate plaid shirts and whom you are still likely to find in the grammar schools of white, middle-class suburbs. I recall spending hours tapping nervously on my black rubber practice pad in the school's mahogany music room, waiting for Mr. Gandy to stride in. I was unable to understand how my tapping was connected to music and particularly to the beautiful marches our parents flocked to hear at the Christmas program. For weeks, though, I obediently kept on, trying to wring some music from my menial labor.

Tapping on the pad was one of those monotonous actions I would learn to associate later with cutting countless pieces of fabric at my father's textile business in the grimy Loop. During the summer, and sometimes during the winter on Saturday, the moment I arrived in the morning I could hear, through the wall, the scissors clucking in the back room. Was it possible that during the weekdays while I was doing push-ups in the gymnasium at school or selling milk in the lunchroom, while I was learning the lines of girls' calves, the people who worked in the back room were doing nothing but cutting and wrapping packages? Or was it possible, really true, that

every night that I drifted into mellifluous dreams, their sons
and cousins had no dreams at all or dreamed of foods they
didn't know the names of? I sent the scissors snickering across
the cloth, flapped back the pieces, slit another piece and
flapped it back until all the pieces in the stack were cut and
folded back, revealing the table on which I had been cutting.
Between each cut, my mind would wander; I would hear myself panting between push-ups, or I would pretend I was serving a life sentence at hard labor, condemned to cut grille cloth
for my entire life.

The days I spent in that back-room atmosphere of blacks
and brown paper, clipboards and hidden snapshots of Marilyn
Monroe's cunt, so full of strangeness, were still boring. I
sought refuge at the water cooler, waiting for the day to give
itself up. After a while, I became a member of the community
and learned the lyrics to the tunes on the spade radio stations
and ate grits with crushed bacon at lunchtime. When I
learned that they often came to work high, I felt even closer.
So much that when I visited them on vacation from school, I
wanted to pretend I had spent the interim shooting up on
the South Side or working in a factory. In the end, though,
they always seemed to know who I was despite the fact that
we shook revolutionary handshakes and they called me
brother. When Franklin told me about how the parking lot
he partly owned on the West Side had been terrorized by the
Blackstone Rangers and he had had to dive behind a car as
they opened up on him with a shotgun, I didn't know how to
react. His nonchalance invited my nervous laughter. There
was a point after which I simply couldn't get any closer to
them. Up to that point, what I really admired in these relationships was the discovery of my flexibility.

Always the boss's son, I was never the son of a boss. I fell in
love with their lives from a distance. I relished stolen free-
doms on the job and encouraged everyone else to take it easy,
as if they could afford to. Once I was even sent home by my
father for curling up among the dusty bolts of material to

read a paperback long after lunch was over. He discovered me when he came back to check on something in the shipping office. I protested; after all, it was clear that reading was more important than cutting. I would make the mistake of thinking that for years to come. The book? The autobiography of Nathan Leopold.

How could I not, at times, be ashamed of the affluence which permitted me to escape these tediums as a way of life? Can it be that I sometimes wished I had been raised in a life in which I had to, was able to, cut cloth forty hours a week? Bourgeois guilt. But, since I had always lived on the other side, I could never cut for a living without being annoyingly self-conscious and literary about it. The understanding, primarily economic and transmitted to me by the events and atmosphere of my youth, that I would not have to do it, made it, in turn, impossible for me to do it.

The drums were a similar experience. I was not forced to play drums. I was already an athlete; I drew, I attended art classes; there were so many other things I was better at, could understand, could be exposed to. The rhythm of the sticks on my pad, incomprehensible and inane, became not an obligation or a fact of life, but merely another option in the permissive illogic of growing up in the suburbs. For, whenever a drum teacher fell out of my life, a baseball coach or eager geometry teacher popped into it.

I was not a kind from the West Side saving up for a practice pad on his way to percussional fame; I was neither hungry nor fanatical. Mom bought me a pad as soon as I expressed idle interest in drums. After a few weeks, I was already concealing my boredom from my beaming mother; then my father came home with a pair of brushes! And then a whole set of drums! By that time, of course, I had already decided drums were not for me, although I did use them for a week or two before my father and brothers, suddenly avid drummers, monopolized them, freeing me to go on to another hobby.

As I knew I could take drums or leave them, as I knew even then that my life didn't exactly enforce diligence or frugality, so I discovered later that cutting grille cloth, like drums, was a good experience and needed to be taken only as seriously as I pleased. Isn't the logic that even bad experiences are good experiences a purely middle-class logic? If we were irrevocably locked inside those bad experiences by poverty or color, they would not be experiences at all, but painful and persistent realities. The element which makes any bad experience good is the fact that I can always choose to return home after each one, after every involvement, home to tell my parents at the dinner table how I was robbed outside Comiskey Park after the doubleheader. It is only because I collected bad experiences like baseball cards that I could show them proudly to my friends.

There was nothing truly impoverished in my adolescence; a tape recording of that period would include no cries of desperation other than those psychic ones we all come to feel regardless of physical comfort. Rousseau speaks of his first indignity, of being accused for a petty crime he didn't commit; the girl in Robert Bresson's *Mouchette* clomps noisily into the classroom in her sabots because she can't afford shoes. I have never been mistaken for the villain. I can only look back to oversights: the time I was at hockey camp in Minnesota. I was skating very poorly, feeling the inside of my right ankle scrape the ice as I made turns. The others noticed and laughed, or else ignored me, confident that I was just an inferior player. A coach took me aside and examined my skates. "My god," he said, "these skates are awful. They're not good enough for a six-year-old!" That night I called my father and was soon in tears over the phone. "Dad," I pleaded, "the coaches all told me I need a new pair of Tacks. They're on sale for thirty-eight dollars." After two days and several phone calls, my parents deferred to my need and I was soon playing a mean left wing, popping in hat tricks the first two games.

My life also seems peculiarly devoid of neighborhood

dramas. The city had preempted potential street fights by sup-
plying us with spacious parks. Yet one thing does come to
mind: There was a family with three sons which lived down
the street. The younger sons' conception of a good time dif-
fered somewhat from the more passive versions favored by my
friends and me. Once, for instance, I was held prisoner in the
attic above their garage for an entire afternoon. I was convinced I was a real captive; I obeyed their modest commands,
was grateful for the small amenities they showed me. They
fed me, showed me dirty photographs. But I was their prisoner and didn't even contemplate escaping. Before nightfall,
they released me to go home to dinner. I was in third grade:
they were in fifth.

Anyway, I remember sitting in their bedroom at a later
date. I was watching them hang little chicks they had received for Christmas. With an Erector set, they had con-
structed a miniature gallows. They marched the chicks up the
steps, daintily holding their little legs, simulating the slow
walk of a condemned prisoner. A small red thread was placed
around their necks. An announcement, an order, or a bene-
diction was given. The trap door opened. The chick struggled; was dead.

Next frame: My life of crime began on a December night
in eighth grade. After a party at a girl's house, six of us, with
varying degrees of conviction, decided to walk down the darkened street to the junior high school. There, we would paint
Class of 67 somewhere on the wall of the school with the
white paint from the hostess's garage. All six of us walked
quietly toward the school, hard snow and ice crunching underneath. No traffic, no lights on in the houses. We carried pails
and long-handled brushes. When we arrived at the school, set
almost luminously in an open space, we halted; our plans gave
way suddenly to fear. Luckily, two boys found the strength to
take the two brushes and the paint and run across the snow
to the front of the building. We other four remained behind,
across the street, huddled together. We talked nervously.

When we looked up, we were stunned to see that Jeff and Stuart had painted Class of 67 in letters seven feet high across the front of the building. We had, at most, expected a modest inscription in the corner; but our crime was committed over the entire face of the main building. I, personally, was stricken. The letters were legible, certainly, except for some drippings. The job had been done quickly, smartly. But the crime was too large! It was too high! I would not have come if I had known it wasn't going to be a tidy crime, committed in the corner by the cafeteria wall.

Eight months later, I was swimming in a pool. August. My mother called me and said the police wanted to see me in the station. My freedom was about to begin. I dried myself; my mother picked me up and drove me to the red brick station house. There, after walking stoically down the long corridor, I was placed in a light green room with a one-way mirror and required to make a full written confession. I felt no guilt; only excitement. Later, the principal of the school called a meeting for all the defendants and their parents. It was ludicrous. The principal, angered beyond composure, shrieked and chastised, meting out a verbal punishment grossly ill-proportioned to the crime. His excesses made us laugh at our transgression, not despise it. One of the boys' fathers, probably the only one who took the principal's tirade seriously, spoke out against him, and for thirty minutes, a battle raged overhead while we boys and girls, smiling at one another across the room, bit our nails.

Two scenes stand out about the whole affair: (1) Coming to school on the first morning of classes after vacation, we saw our creation in broad daylight. What had looked so other-worldly late on a snowy evening, those tall, white letters and the snow and cold air, what had seemed so daring, particularly with girls involved and the promise of postmisdemeanor affections, was now mundane. It looked too much like other crimes we had observed on movie theaters and high schools. (Two of the others involved in the caper were destined to work off this disappointment, a year later, by pulling an even bigger job at the Alcyon Theater in town, but I was destined to live with it longer.) But it was my crime and I was duly proud, shivering as I walked past it into the school. For days, kids spoke of it, wondering who had done it. I affected an exaggerated air of normalcy and strolled through the halls, completely innocent. (2) But it really wasn't my crime. The police were kind enough to call me an accomplice because I had stood on the side and done nothing to prevent it, but I felt I was even less than that. My heart was not in the act at all. I had had no intention of doing the painting, but was too frightened to run. I remember standing in the cold with two girls and a boy while we watched the others put the last touches on the 7. That pose seems paradigmatic; it has become a familiar one. Caught hopelessly somewhere between the idea and the act.

So the greatest affluence may not have been money itself, but one of its effects: the affluence of choice, of selecting with impunity. In the town I lived in, I could never really make a wrong turn. All the streets were good-looking and all the lawns were manicured. It was an affluence that made some smugly secure, but bestowed others with a sense of alternative: opportunity was interpreted as a chance to be flexible. Free of the necessary occupation, one could learn to be discriminating, to acknowledge a variety of methods, not to resign oneself to an inherited style. And while this sort of affluence hardly endeared those who didn't have it to a cultural revolution, it was still one of the few advantages that could be gleaned from a' middle-class background that had preempted so many subtler decisions. Surely, one had the opportunity to become a Minuteman or a Bircher, but choice itself seemed to be a radical phenomenon and the possibilities reached endlessly in the other direction.

But more and more this freedom of choice seemed to be illusory, operating successfully only until we were faced with terrifying decisions, when we were immobilized by the very fact that we had options. Constant choice proved itself to be static.

I know that man riding the elevator to the thirty-sixth floor. He attracts my attention because it may have been his only ambition to fall into this previously established rhythm; his dress may be a uniform, as if wearing suits is an occupational imperative. He enunciates his fate only in the form of easy answers, not questions. Of course, I am sympathetic to his situation, but equally so to mine: I must save myself from *his* errors before I have the opportunity to make them. His hands remind him so much of staple removers that he can no longer play the piano.

We had to continue to inform ourselves of the infinite possibilities in a pluralist society and exercise those possibilities on a personal level by experimenting with as many sensory and experiential options as we could.

The opulence of life in the suburbs was not without its essential crises, of course. Because the principles of pain and pleasure often appeared to operate the same for kids everywhere, observing a relativity while disregarding the larger economic context, for years I probably experienced emotions which could not have been more or less intense than those felt by a boy in the ghetto. When I didn't get the Pontiac on an evening I needed it, were my feelings that much different from a ghetto kid's going without dinner for still another night? We learned to adjust our hopes and fears to the type of life at hand, to react according to the vicissitudes we have learned to expect.

The happiness of my adolescence was more often modulated, rather than by material/physical comfort, by sensations whose autonomous beauty encouraged me to confront the dullness of their context. I was overjoyed by those moments when I suddenly felt free of my antagonists. When I was alone, underneath a viaduct in Montreal on June 11. When I read something that instantaneously seemed to decipher the events of my life. A configuration of clouds. An object deposited somewhere on the earth recalled to me the possibilities of living. I looked for breathing space; it was a little room that made me happy for a moment, room located between the thing and its finality. More space between hours, between cars, between thoughts. I was a little familiar with the tendency of history; I had already read the memoirs of my own life, and I hoped that the pattern established was not irreversible.

For two years, during sixth and seventh grades, I attended dancing school at the junior high. Mr. Valez, the dance instructor whose toupee had once fallen off while he attempted to demonstrate the boxstep, was a hot-blooded tango aficionado. Side-step, side-step, step-back. SIDE-step, SIDE-step, step-BACK; that was the jitterbug. Oh, but it was more than that; we would drive our feet pneumatically into the floor, rocking and swaying, digging and doing, feeling good, our hair shiny, our parts an inch wide. We stylized it, made it our own, became aware of its subtleties. Not until we learned big words and began to buy our own clothes did we personalize our lives as much as when we jitterbugged. Even the guys who looked bad looked good.

Mostly, though, our energies were restricted to slow stuff, and all of us boys would wait to dance with certain girls who were known to be precociously well developed. How we would love to feel their pert breasts against our corduroy jackets. Every few minutes, Mr. Valez announced, "Everyone move one place to the right!" and we would move on to our next partner; for almost two years, every time he said that, I would respond, knowing I was getting closer to the girls I loved to hold. One night in the spring of seventh grade, we had just finished a waltz step and Mr. Valez announced, "Everyone move one place to the right!" Suddenly, for the first time in two years, I felt a certain revulsion. For the first time in two years, I did not want to move one place to my

right. As Ronnie and Ed, Cathy and Melinda, slid across the
floor to meet their new partners, I remained where I was,
motionless, adamant, in the gymnasium of a junior high
school in the suburb of a city in the country that gave the
world the jitterbug.

4. A Note on my American Heritage

Here's a trick that was played on me. Just as I possessed the
ability to strike fear into the hearts and parts of policemen,
pharmacists, particularly my parents, there was something in
me which was afraid of them—no, rather than feared, revered
them and their histories. Aware of the toil of their lives, my
leisures became a burden and my neuroses something less exciting than romantic deviations. I was awed by their heritage;
I was surprised, as an adolescent, to be told that it was also
mine. I could hardly believe how they could have created, at
least been absorbed by, a stratum of society so repellent that
I often longed for the re-creation of their youths. When I see
carcasses and dripping legs of beef pulled off the backs of
trucks, I am immediately reminded of my grandfather's boy-
hood in Eastern Europe, as if I had been his grandson even
then. Quite frankly, Oscar Mayer's pimento-and-olive loaf
weighs me down. I do not love their heritage as inviolable traditions, but as a succession of images tightened into a ball, in-
vincible.

Could it be that some of the pretty parcels of contempt
that I had been sending to my elders were being returned to
me unopened as small packages of guilt? Now and then, I
would have consented to renounce all my privileges and opportunities if that would have permitted me the same soiled
adolescence as my predecessors. I longed for a pack of Luckies
at Ashland and Division, behind the shoe store.

My obsession was with another age that seemed to require
so much more of the instincts. The age I found myself in not
only suffered from a severe dissociation of mind and body,

but appeared incapable of serving either. Our bodies, victims of bad air, unsavory vegetables, and sexual partners who had discovered satisfaction without ever having discovered desire, puckered. As for our minds, they were well-fed, but kept indoors. We received educations and acquired a cosmic awareness which exceeded the world's ability to make them useful. Education was a deceptive medium because it revealed to us in its course the infinite possibility for creation and peace, and escorted us into a society which often defied us to aspire. For those who didn't realize this, for those seduced by their own creativity and visions, the world's negligence of them would come as a disturbing surprise. Those who already understood that they would not be honored for their dreams began to make plans which excluded the world they were brought up in. They were giving us knowledge, but denying us its real application: they were getting us hot, then they were taking away our women.

My grandfather, soon after the death of his wife, accompanied me and the dog to the vet's. "You know when I had my first woman?" he asked as I turned off the highway. I instinctively braked a little, anxiously, always bitter that suburban life had painfully prolonged my virginity. I was afraid to look at him across the seat.

"When I was thirteen," he smiled broadly. I came to a full stop.

"Oh, yeah?" I said, choking on something that was both sweet and pungent.

"Sure," he said, "sure. I remember it like it was today. She was a Jewish girl. I gave her half a buck. My friends told me about her and I went to her and she was angry that I was so young. You know, she didn't think I was old enough. When I was older, fifteen, there were always women at the dances. Every weekend we used to go to the dances."

Now, I would give away a lot to have been laid at thirteen, or even fifteen, on the untidy West Side of Chicago. I can see myself, wearing a cap and a pair of dongola nullifiers, clutching two quarters, ketchup under my nails. Eternal joy and manhood! Sometimes, this is all I ask.

My grandmother on the other side told us as we sat around —old aunts gathered too, tottering in their seats—at my uncle's house a few days after her husband died: "Hymie," she said. "Hymie. Hymie, he was a great man. Sometimes, six and seven times a night!" It's not that I was already feeling impotent, nor is it that sex is the best thing of all (although, in times of crises, statistics favor this conclusion), but that these seemed to be such handsome memories; soiled, but untinged by intimations of death. I did not want to look back and see busts, gas, riots, suicides, if I was not by then living in a world made better by these sacrifices. I didn't want the excruciating wisdom we had at such an early age to be for nothing. The pain of their youths was different, not necessarily better or worse, but closer to the earth and the grocery stores on the frayed edges of Chicago.

> . . . Now I can drive back
> Home past wreck and car lot, past shack
> Slum and steelmill reddening the skies,
> Past drive-ins, the hot pits where our teens
> Fingerfuck and that huge screen's
> Images fill their vacant eyes.
> —W. D. Snodgrass, *After Experience* *

A couple of years ago, I was home from college, watching TV idly on a Saturday night; I was alone, pulling on a cigarette from the package of Salems my mother keeps in the freezer for guests who smoke. I was home, but further away from home than ever before. Finally, I turned off the TV and jumped into the car, heading for McDonald's. I drove west, watching the flattened suburbs smooth entirely into prairie after a few miles. I did not want a fish fillet sandwich. I did

* From "A Friend" in *After Experience* by W. D. Snodgrass. Copyrighted © 1968 by W. D. Snodgrass. Reprinted by permission of Harper & Row, Publishers, Inc.

not even want to go to McDonald's. In this culture, even the atrocities for which I have no real use, I still find myself observing as spectacles. I parked in the lot and bought a fish fillet sandwich. The November evening was black and cool and the lot was swarming with high school students, many of them propping their legs confidently on fenders. Above everything that grated, there was an insouciance that charmed me.

Walking back to my car I passed a parked Mustang. In the front seat were a high school boy and his girl. On the seat lay crumpled french fries' bags and the crisp plastic tops to carry-out drink containers. The boy and girl had finished eating and were listening to the radio, which transported some ridiculous song out into the lot. The boy, looking out the window, maybe at me, was at the same time putting his hand on the girl's breast. He fumbled for some meat through her thick padded bra as they sat amidst the debris of their recent meal. The girl, who wore a dotted culotte dress, the kind that makes it impossible for guys to get into their pants, took hold of his wrist and wrenched his hand away; it was so obviously a battle in which no one had won. I walked back quietly to my car.

Something was wrong. The metal prongs the guy used inside the drive-in to pinch a cluster of oily fries before dropping them into a bag were all wrong. Two days later, flying back to school, I sat next to a girl. She was all right and I wanted to talk to her. As always when I want to talk to a strange girl, the first voice I hear is not mine, but that of the narrator in a novel. "He saw her next to him in the seat. He looked out of the corner of his eye. Outside the airplane window, the orange sun shone magnificently. She wore a sleeveless blouse which revealed her tan, sun-flecked shoulders. She was probably a girl who spent her summers lolling on the beach at Sag Harbor. He lifted his. . . ." Usually, you can ask for a cigarette, but I don't really smoke and it's a stupid line. I turned to her finally after the in-flight meal and said, "It's fortunate we have teeth, don't you think?" She turned slightly toward me, almost as if she were going to fall over in my lap, and then slumped back in her seat. She was silent until we touched down, when she asked if I might get her coat for her from the overhead rack.

My family doesn't celebrate Christmas, Easter, Memorial Day, or the President's national days of prayer. Birthdays rarely find a quorum of the members at home and pass unnoticed. The difficulty of circumstance has always made ritual next to impossible. Except for Thanksgivings. On Thanksgiving, we have often all wandered back home for the weekend to gather around the altar of our past. We do not celebrate it at all. It's just the time when we all seem to be there. I remember how quickly they came, creeping up like Miss America contests which, like Thanksgivings, are only supposed to take place once a year. Yet, it seems like every few months that Bert Parks asks us to stand by for the special event. There must have been twelve or fifteen Thanksgivings in the last five years.

They begin at the airport. Airports are to me what the tower must have been to Jung. "In the tower at Bollingen, it was as if you lived in many centuries simultaneously . . . there is very little to suggest the present." Similarly, the airport, despite its vulgar reminders of modernity, suggests not the present, but the past and future, departure and arrival, fused by timeless and landless idea of motion. I remember the bus trips between Providence and Boston late at night, drawing on a small cigar and trying to make out the old textile mills and warehouses along 95. Sensations of all tenses converging at once, there is no use attempting to orchestrate the past, present, and future. Sequences disobey and collapse. Miles consume each other without consuming time or distance. Pawtucket appears in a dream beyond a trestle; darkened sporting goods stores come alive; the fielders' gloves start talking, flapping their large leather lips. In the seat next to me, a man sleeps with his mouth open. Time edges backward, ap-

proaching a point in the future. It is like the first few moments after you awake in the morning, when there are no
thoughts of the present, only the raveled ends of dreams or the
day ahead. Those moments are timeless transitions from one
level of consciousness to another as airports and buses are the
cluttered fluorescent interfusions of two clocks and places.

Thanksgiving morning, asleep, in a still, milky light. My
mother wades through the room to wake me. I hear the dog
downstairs and a motorcycle start down the street. I feel im-
munized against all diseases of the head; I stretch and dress
slowly as the quiet and ignorant house folds over me.

My brothers and I bound downstairs to the breakfast table.
There is thick bacon, cream cheese, eggs, tomatoes, chives,
potatoes, fish, orange juice, coffee, rolls, kippers. Mother med-
dles with pots at the stove. Sometimes, it seems that we all
conserve our radiance for certain mornings. Father lopes down
to join us in his pajamas. A rivulet of toothpaste runs from the
corner of his mouth, but no one tells him to wipe it off. Someone expels emphatic gas and we begin to eat. My sister, maybe
twelve or thirteen in her light blue nightie, puts her hand in
the cream cheese. We are happy to be caught in our under-
pants, with marmalade on our wrists.

Thanksgiving in late November: the funneling of disparate
images into the single moment of a weekend, a symbol in an
eclectic history, the recurring dream. Anesthetized by the
past, I become it finally, a nine-year-old petting the dog on the
carpet. Annie, the big beautiful black woman who rocked me
in my cradle singing songs with religious words in them, has
come up from the city for the occasion. We used to sit in the
kitchen on days when I stayed home sick from grammar
school. She would tell me about the farms in Mississippi and
God. She was thirteen when she was married. When I was
thirteen, I went down to her apartment on the South Side. I
was hurt by its poverty. It was one of many subdivided units
on the floor. I asked, why do people go to the bathroom in
the hallway? She had squeezed a houseful of articles into two

small rooms. The broken TV rested on top of the refrigerator. Chairs and tables competed for space with the stove. If
there were windows, they were covered up by cupboards or
calendars from insurance companies. Were the farms in Mississippi like this too? It was my first exposure to a measure of
poverty; my vocabulary of experience was improving, and after
a while I learned to use big words without having any idea
what they meant. Now, at Thanksgiving dinner, we talked
and laughed together. Suddenly, I wanted to be in her arms
again, to know of nothing but her crisp white uniform and
mammoth breast.

"You got to be a do-right man to make us women do right,"
she said. "Pass the cranberry sauce." Did she know twenty
years ago when she held me that she'd be sitting across from
me today, her hair combed grayly back? Did she know then
what I'd look like and say, whether my beard would be this
heavy, and whether I still thought of God?

The few moments when I awake from this recurring dream,
I am afraid and small. At three in the morning Saturday, after
a date with an old girl friend, I park the car in the garage and
get out. There isn't a light on in the house. I have never seen
the trees in the yard so thin. A cold wind exhales the sky. My
footsteps on the cement garage floor frighten me, as though
they were a stranger's, approaching menacingly from behind.
I turn around, expecting to find a cab driver in a sweater or
an austere Eastern European with rimless glasses. I am tall
and old and hungry. In the lobby of a movie theater, I have a
look specially engineered for the moment. But in garages at
night, I look frightened, keeping my distance, leery of rakes
and whisk brooms. I am far away from my friends, my family,
myself. When I think that they are only beginning, why do
so many histories seem to have completed themselves? I take
off my coat and enter the house. The refrigerator hums nervously in the kitchen; my family and the weekend guests
dream uneasily upstairs. Good night.

It is Sunday morning, summer. Mother shakes me from my soft sleep. "Dad just called," she says. "Grandpa died this morning." It is the first thing I have ever lost. "Oh, god," I murmur. When we call my brother in Brazil the next day, his voice carries huskily across the continents: "Oh, god." After his tiring decade of strokes and complications, Grandpa finally found a finale. Father would tell us, when he arrived at the airport with grandma, how they used a rude metal clamp to keep grandpa's mouth open so that they could lower an air pipe down his throat. For the last few days, nurses squeezed a red rubber ball to keep him alive. A futile gesture, it simply meant that people ought to live. At least, I think to myself, it is a rubber ball and not a machine with too many moving parts. For the strong and simple man who invented Quench-Aid and planted dusty grocery stores all over Chicago, it is good it was a rubber ball.

He dominated his own funeral, even though they used some contraption to lower his casket into the ground. At the funeral of my grandmother on the other side a year and a half later, it was different. The squat red-brick chapel was across from not one but two car washes. All day long, the autos underwent their soapy sanctification. Inside the chapel, the director bowed, and plastic ferns nodded in every corner. When the mourners came, they seemed out of place. Could it be possible they were feeling a real solemnity that every detail in the chapel failed to substantiate—the aluminum coffee urns and the matchbooks engraved with the name of the chapel, the decor like that of a delicatessen, the machines for taking the casket here and there? Like so much else in my grandmother's life, that was not in her favor, nor ours. The only thing truly in her behalf was the closed casket, keeping us from her ineffable face and her from life's erroneous commodities.

In the powder room, I relieved myself. With my instrument I carefully wrote fuck you in urine on the bottom of the up-lifted toilet seat. As I washed my hands, goosing the soap, relatives came in without knocking.

"The rabbi gave a nice little speech, I think!"
"So beautiful."
"I want it should be so nice for me."

I placed one hand on top of the dead head and with the other I rubbed at the waxy face. The paint was coming off all right—and the filler under the cheeks was shifting around. A horrible outcry went up, my mother's and several others, "Stop it!" "Stop him!" I gripped the collar of her velvet dress and gave a terrific yank. All her pearls went flying, and the screams redoubled, with an admixture of horror, for my grandmother's gray skin had come into view, her scrawny collarbones and pathetic ribs. And now I knew the appropriate rites: simple death; death and decomposition; the smell of the flesh; vomiting; rage. These would be my ceremony.
—George Dennison, *On Being a Son*

The grief goes out of me sometimes. I am sorry. But I cannot cry. We are not mourners; we are a *minyon* of Methodists humming Yiddish songs in the English translation. I am not solemn. I only have a terrible longing for solemnity.

Cultivated people go to a melodrama to hiss the villain with an air of condescension: they are making a point of fact that they cannot take his villainy seriously. We have here a type of irony which corresponds to that of two other major arts of the ironic age, advertising and propaganda. These arts pretend to address themselves seriously to a subliminal audience of cretins . . . which is assumed to be simple minded enough to accept at their face value the statements made about the purity of a soap or a government's motives. The rest of us, realizing that irony never says precisely what it means, takes these arts ironically, or, at least, regards them with a strong sense of the unreality of the irony involved.
—Northrup Frye, *Anatomy of Criticism*

For as long as I can remember, we have been going to funerals, sock-hops, and rallies, only to find ourselves heckling the funeral directors, disk jockeys, and political whores who make it their business to rob the occasions of their meaning.

The men who run this country have watched too many "Ozzie and Harriet" shows. Ruling their household with anachronisms, they are forever struggling up toward the presidency of the PTA. They presuppose the complacency, the fatuity, of another era, and in the process, they detain history. They are truly sorry we haven't turned out like Ricky and Dave.

Duplicity is contagious, and much propaganda developed within the movement. There are too many attempts to confuse the substance of the so-called counterculture with its aura. The line between hippie and hippie entrepreneur, the line between honest radical and man in bell-bottoms, was blurred. In certain issues of *The Village Voice*, there was an ad depicting two beautiful twenty-year-olds in the latest hip fashions. He had his hand lovingly on her shoulder; no cold turkeys for them. The bold type read: Wear Your Convictions. And the ad continued: "Duds to do that thing, and make you look on the outside the way you feel on the inside. . . . Earth clothes to cover your body and feed your head." If the mass-produced hip clothes these two wore expressed any conviction, it was the one that you can buy your hip-ness at Sears Roebuck or the latest boutique. The fact that too many people were doing precisely that, letting their clothes feed their heads, mistaking the appearance of flare pants on their legs for the appearance of good images on their screens troubled whatever movement we could call our own. There are ways to express your convictions on and with your body, but they certainly aren't by following this ad. Dressing is a whole aesthetic, but it is not immediate proof of substantive convictions.

In *The Making of a Counter Culture*, Theodore Roszak has reiterated the old complaint: "It is the cultural experimentation of the young that often runs the worst risk of commercial verminization—and so of having the force of its dissent dissipated. It is the cultural experiments that draw the giddy interest of just those middle-class swingers who are the bastion of the technocratic order."

"The sad truth is," [the *Saturday Evening Post*] said in the au-
tumn of 1931, "that the Village was a flop." Perhaps it was
true that the Village was moribund . . . it was dying of success. It was dying because it became so popular . . . because
women smoked cigarettes on the streets of the Bronx, drank
gin cocktails in Omaha and had perfectly swell parties in Se-
attle and Middletown—in other words, because American
business and the whole of middle-class America had been
going Greenwich Village.

—Malcolm Cowley, *Exile's Return*

It seemed almost necessary to disagree with Malcolm Cowley that if the countercultural Village was dying, it was dying
of success. Its ability to superficially influence the middle
class was hardly a sign of its success. But the fact that execu-
tives now wore bell-bottoms or that adults are heard to murmur at cocktail parties, "Far out," only became destructive
when their appropriation of our fads affected our definition
of those fads. We were enervated by their mimicry only when
we confused their meanings with ours. If we could not retain
our fads and experimentations intact despite commercializa-
tion, they were apparently not very healthy in the first place.

What do funerals and political demonstrations have in
common? For me, they both effectively obscure their purposes. It is hard to think of death at funerals and to think of
political rage at demonstrations. There is something in the
way they are done that deflates them. At funerals I think of
coffee urns and car washes; at demonstrations, of Boeing 747s
and dinner.

I was not fond of history. If I ignored, disrespected, even
blasphemed it, that was because of this: I never learned the
lessons of history; I was, instead, taught only its tedious
chronology, taught that the parade of events and names is, in
itself, an incredible thing. Maybe it was my fault for not
grasping what secret the congestion of data concealed. When

I was young and my family took a car trip around the Great Lakes, we passed time by playing "Beaver!" trying to be the first to cry out "Beaver!" when we spotted the type of car we had designated as It. The endless procession of passing cars meant nothing. What thrilled us, and made the game, was only the recurrence of green Buicks and white Ramblers. What of the continuum between Father Girard of eighteenth-century France who spent much of his time impregnating the mademoiselles of his flock, and our own Charles Manson? Did Machiavelli's son share his father's politics? From the beginning, history must be taught by argument and content, not by decade. What of the rhythms of history? In our efforts to codify the past, we have ignored the terrible insistence of to-day's history to be recognized and amended. From grand-parents to Thanksgiving to education, we must free ourselves from the rote and obligations of history, and learn the dignities of our own contemporaneousness. As much time as we spend in vast supermarkets, we never realized that our tradition is also an A & P. Roaming the infinite aisles, we take only what we want and only what we need.

During the 1968 French Revolution, rigid class distinctions melted. Suddenly, teachers, parents, custodians, and functionaries all got together to discuss the process of education. Workers and capitalists found themselves talking politics over Pernod. Whether the revolution failed or not (the medium of government-owned television did more than anything else to undo successes), the French people momentarily relearned oral communication. During the Harvard strikes in 1969 and 1970, some of us relearned it too, but so momentarily that now we wonder whether the lessons ever took place. We faintly recall that we once made love to the proposition that sometimes we get to pull our own triggers. At those hiatuses in the educational process, it becomes possible to relax. The Problem becomes one of how to achieve an honest grace, everyday, at Burger King, how to maintain poise at the inauguration of still another President: how to ingest polluted air and lies and exhale a meager truth.

I lived in two worlds, a little like Tonio Kröger. Despite my existential impulses, I was still the beneficiary, at least the ardent observer of a beautified way of life which generously bestowed its gifts of blemish cream, loosened inhibitions, material accessibility, and the promise of early notoriety in a society that both flaunted and flagellated its dearest youngsters. Pop culture provided me with the gestures of human response, but left me unable to master moments of real intimacy.

Even though I couldn't get enough of alienation, I still found myself in the mainstreams I had hoped I had paddled out of. This was due, in part, to cowardice, a fear of disaffiliating myself from sources I might need when the gunfire breaks out. The ambiguity of my life was also responsible; being what I was, I felt the disparity between America's taste in culture and politics and mine. Yet not being stupid, I could not always refuse the gifts that society insisted on giving me. When a pimple appeared on my forehead, I was immediately faced with a moral decision. Should I treat it with a special cream or encourage it to reach a natural death. There is something very beautiful about certain pimples, yet I could have so easily disposed of it with a new product, as easily as sponging a stain off a linoleum floor.

Many skeptics would like to think that radicals' compliance with some of the lesser plots of our culture (TV, El Marko pens, media publicity, complexion ointments, scholarships) proves their insincerity. But to doubt a radical's general rejection of his culture the moment he succumbs to a particular is only the hasty criticism of anxious liberals to his right. The occupation of radicals with Americanisms is far from hypocrisy or weakness. For instance, the President may prefer baseball to taking care of business. He may, in fact, watch the Ohio State–Purdue football game on TV rather than acknowledge a massive political demonstration in his own backyard. Nixon's actions assure the silent majority he will not be touched by either protests, youngsters, or intellectuals. "I'm American, you can bet," he says between halves. Whereas Nixon implies a cock-eyed set of priorities in which sports is more American than dissent, hence, more important, the radical who is also a baseball fan does not overestimate its importance nor let it get in the way of more meaningful pastimes.

By accepting baseball (or rodeos or Neil Sedaka) as part of his ethos, the radical doesn't necessarily come off as a parttime or inauthentic one, but often the opposite. By accommodating both baseball and radical action in his life-style, he shows himself to possess that radical instinct, a cultural generosity, that Nixon never dreamed of. That is, not to categorically reject all things foreign to one's dogma, but to engage in activities outside the range of one's politics, but within the scope of one's love.

In the suburbs, surrounded by the products of technology, it was easy to acquire a superficial distaste for the stuff. Instead of demanding the newest Schwinn on the market, I acquired an affinity for old pens, pocketing them at large chain stores. Also for cheap wine-soaked cigars and Progresso eggplant appetizer. Forced by technology to find my happiness in the most obscure regions, I often discovered it in the elements that technology had superseded—antiquated movie theaters with small screens where I could commentate raucously on the movie from the depths of the balcony. In the new theaters, so well equipped and capacious they are hardly distinguishable from airports, ushers constantly scan the seats with their officious flashlights, hunting offenders whose crimes were once the hidden delights of the cinematic experience. The idea of rolling your own with Bull Durham, of mastering even that modest skill, appealed. I remember the defiant pleasure I derived from wearing sloppy clothes in a scrupulously attired suburb.

But these gestures, it became clear, hardly constituted an

overthrow of the technocratic state. Even my friend who viciously ripped down two junior high school clocks from the
wall in seventh grade ended up devising an unbeatable Tic-
Tac-Toe computer a year later. As for me, I, did not defy
technology so much as identify with an earlier stage in its
growth. Technology was scarcely affronted by my superficial
impudence, which amounted to nothing less than capitula-
tion; technology thrives particularly on victims who dress their
commitment to it as art or eccentricity.

Technology has obviated so many fundamental skills and
processes that I have become almost afraid to use my hands.
On the street, they feel large and gangly at my sides. Acquiring
the simplest skills—cooking, planting, carpentry, standing
gracefully—forces me to momentarily step out of the available
urban world. Whether the electronic age retribalizes us all to
the point where we can unself-consciously master them remains to be seen. Until then, I will have to make aggressive
efforts to avoid the interference of machines. The larger technology's domain becomes, the more I search for pleasures outside of it, crowding into the last few spaces. But geographical
and spiritual space is running out; every time we stretch, our
arms hit some neighboring idiocy.

5. My Autobiography

I see my growing up as a process of diminishing space. The
population explosion began to manifest itself on a subtle scale.
When I was nine and a half, I was a summer camper, breathing easily in dark green Wisconsin, although I only stayed
four weeks before my parents rescued me from the nightmare
of early solitude. Then I was a teenager whose blemishes were
not so much facial as social; I was alternately arrogant and
withdrawn, self-possessed and dispossessed. Already, people
were larger and classrooms were smaller.

During the summers I played baseball, batting seventh
those damp days on the rural diamonds whose fenceless out-

fields stretched to the Midwestern horizon, taking neighboring states with them. Looking back, I was embarrassingly close to America. But I admit my closeness to her body warmed me. I wondered if it was right for a baseball player to write poetry— no, I should say I knew it was right for a young poet to play first base. Each poem I wrote helped to unravel my anxieties. I discovered metaphors that exposed the falsehoods of my adolescence. I grew apart, cherishing my literary alienation; somehow, I continued to play baseball, and much else besides. Somehow I learned to live with a tenuous schizophrenia. While the other infielders talked it up during the game, I recited the names of the English Romantics. I have a newspaper clipping about the clutch double I once hit in a tournament. To tell the truth, my name is unfamiliar to me in the column of type, my past no longer recognizable.

In between stanzas, I watched TV telecasts of major league games. I'll always recall the fouls behind the plate, arching up and back toward the broadcast area. Scorecards rustle and folding chairs collapse: the announcer, in moist frenzy, ducks and sighs into the mike: "Wow, folks! That one was almost up here in the booth!"

Later, I was a college freshman, confined both by my dormitory cubicle and my impatience. I spent two summers as an assistant editor at a fashionable (not fashion) magazine, where I contracted a disease or two, but managed to identify and immunize myself against others. I was introduced to the fragrant world of secretaries and associate editors. Often, I would have to escape the editorial offices, well lubricated with lip gloss and the oils of social courtesy, and eat alone at El Taco Loco, a small Mexican restaurant with bright orange walls. There, everyone chattered in Spanish and ate lumpy servings of guacamole from paper plates. Next year? I might be back at first base. Or the operator of a Laundromat. I might be an apprentice chef, I don't know. I'm a little off balance.

Me and my friends, we no longer profess any graces; footwork around the bag has become too difficult. A cop's stick almost comes down on my head. It's all I can do, summoning lost agility, to get out of the way. I flee to the outer edges of the conflict where I stop for a root beer. Settling back in the cafeteria, I sigh. That one was almost up here in our booth.

.

Deedily Deedily Dee:
Nonaffluent Materialism

1. I have dirtied all my poems with objects. I have soiled all my objects by writing odes to them. I would like to call you now because I am the last person in the world you expect to hear from, but the phone apparatus have good conversations of their own, talking tenderly to one another long distance, late at night. When our cars pull abreast at red lights, they turn to each other and whinny, like horses. We can't see their headlights flicker softly. We are listening to our car radios which are turned all the way up. When I turn the radio down, I look at the other person in the front seat and say resonantly: "I would like you to call this number when your rugs and carpets need cleaning."

If we lower the radio at night, we can hear paint guns in bumper shops French-kissing with vibrant saliva. Garden hoses commit acts which were once considered by us to be obscene, but which we now only find inconvenient or uncomfortable. On the beaches after curfew, dunes undulate together, getting sand in their private parts. The sky changes its direction. In stationery stores, get-well cards breathe their messages to each other while our backs are turned.

The street I live on feels itself moving through the town, feels the slight acclivity as it crosses the tracks. It feels itself turn right and left, widening; it enjoys the smooth weight of fast cars and the radiance of sunny days; it has a definite preference for fair weather. The automobiles insist that the road is there for them, but the road knows better and turns calmly right, skidding into the business district.

I have thought that mechanical objects existed for my use. I believed that I activated the blender by turning the switch, that it was grateful for the life I granted it each time I decided to make a malted milk. I believed that my ball-point pen came to its consciousness in my hand. I deemed neither the blender capable of internal monologue nor the ball-point capable of penning notes to itself. I was incredulous when I watched Walt Disney's version of the *Sorcerer's Apprentice*; I scoffed at a cartoon in which the toys in a toy shop came alive at night to play, and resumed their poses only at the moment the shopkeeper entered in the morning. I failed to see the paradigm in the movie *The Incredible Shrinking Man* when the protagonist, reduced to bite size, struggles to operate a pair of scissors.

It is not often that I have shown a new pair of shoes to a friend and said, "This is a wonderful pair of shoes," without meaning "This is a wonderful pair of shoes for me to wear, don't you think?" or "These will look swell on me" and put them down on the floor to admire them for being shoes. When I was very young, I remember getting presents which I loved for what they were, not what they did. My innocence of functions saved me from abusing the gifts. I recall being afraid to touch a stuffed seal in the morning when I saw it on my dresser, afraid that as soon as my intentions penetrated its field of autonomy, it would be debased, no longer enchanting as an object that provoked the interference of my senses at the same time that it prohibited it. As much as I wished to reach out of bed and grab the seal, I understood the risks involved. If I touched it and brought it into bed with me, it would become *my* seal, and submit to my interpretation of it. I preferred to let it remain on the bedstand, apart, *the* seal, on its own territory. I would almost be afraid to look at its hazy form as though I were in danger of staring it into banality. Only if I took quick glances at it, pulling the covers just below my eyes, did it retain its *sealness* and its meaning, not meaning so much as being. To retain its sealness, I had to keep my distance. As soon as our circles intersected, the seal merged part of its sealness with whatever I was and, of course, lost that quality which captivated me for long morning minutes as I huddled in bed. Eventually, I could no longer stand it and claimed possession of the seal, sweeping it off my bedstand and onto the floor where the seal and I entered the other's world, mingled beings, where we combined and compromised uniquenesses.

Later, I remember a green hillside in eastern France. I stood at the edge of a pasture, filled with heifers, that sloped down under an old aqueduct and spread out into an expansive panorama of brown green and yellow green fields and dark green copses and black thickets and a small bridge on the right and a small train station tucked in the corner of a knoll. I followed a dirt road with my eyes as it carved its way through a forest and behind hills, reappearing in the distance as a fine gray strip running through muted fields which borrowed colors from each other and finally became one hue as they climbed to a crest that concealed the horizon.

It was a scene with many dimensions, that described space in many different ways and for many miles. It was hardly a sight that asked for interpretation or judgment, that even required a spectator. It was a scene so incontestably arranged, so powerful, that it was almost an affront to observe it. I felt the hostility of even the heifers as I edged down the slope.

I sat down in the pasture, but had already become irrevocably part of the scene. Immediately, I discredited it, organized it around myself; I was Wallace Stevens's intrusive jar in Tennessee. My hand in front of my face consumed half of the landscape; my right foot blotted out the train station. As I moved my hand in front of me, its proportion to the scene altered radically, frantically. Everything else that was part of the scene moved together, observing together the laws of perspective; but my hand observed its own impudent rules, as did my body. The foreign object I had introduced when I walked into the picture made it impossible for the French hillside to retain its character.

The project of merging entities entailed a compromise it was often not worth making. No one and nothing retained its singularity in joint enterprise. Even worse, many beautiful objects and people suffered the loss of their one great attribute, solitude.

2. After those days ended, when I unconsciously respected objects and the lives they led, it became harder for me to keep my distance. I was always interfering with them, reaching for them, dragging them into the realm of my possession. I was inclined to forget the paradox that in order to be close to objects, one must keep his distance. Objects should be prized without being possessed. They can be related to only if permitted room in which to be themselves.

The desire for true familiarity with objects was readily exchanged for the desire only to command them. I demanded that my electric toothbrush get my teeth cleaner than ever before, and when my dentist discovered just as much corrosion as before, I wanted to destroy the machine. When a poem which I expected to perform violently upon my senses failed to arouse me, I wanted to seize it by the octave and scream, "Evoke! Evoke!"

> Private property has made us so stupid and partial that an object is only ours when we have it, when it exists for us as capital or when it is directly eaten, drunk, worn, inhabited, etc., in short, utilized in some way.
> —Karl Marx, *Economical and Philosophical Manuscripts*

Hannah Arendt in *Between Past and Future* speaks of the German origin of the word *philistine*: "It designated a mentality which judged everything in terms of immediate usefulness and 'material value' and hence had no regard for such useless objects and occupations as are implied in culture and art."

The necessity of seeing objects as self-sufficient entities, as aesthetic particulars, does not mean that their function must be ignored totally. It simply means that an object should not be defined by the function or the efficiency of the function. A fork, then, is not a pronged utensil used to spear food, an instrument for eating. A fork requires a more specific definition, a description which alludes to the fork's place in the physical world. After all, if we were to define every object by its function, we would soon run into difficulty. Mud, for instance. Granted, spatula, carburetor, and peninsula would not give us much trouble.

Our collective insensitivity to objects is underlined by our habit of condemning a person for treating another "like an object." Admittedly, there are ways in which we have tried to consider objects apart from their functional context, but we have always had ulterior motives. Three instances come to mind. We make collections:

> Everywhere there are people collecting things. There are the petrophiles who collect stones, the nicophiles who collect cigarette packets, the vitophiles who collect cigar bands. The tyrosemiophiles who collect cheese labels . . . There are the transatlanto-nautophiles who collect ocean liners, the albinelephantophiles who collect white elephants, and the motoroscaphocadillacophiles who collect engines of American cars adapted as outboard motors. There are the philopantophiles who collect collections.
>
> —J. M. G. Le Clézio, *Terra Amata*

Yet when we collect, we are not so much interested in what we are collecting, in whether it is red or sharp, as in how much of it we can find to collect. If we are trying to organize the world, to order our lives, by gathering everything of the same kind to put in boxes and on chains, we have nonetheless failed to make an aesthetic statement about what we collect. Most casual collections are merely personal efforts to unclutter a world cluttered with countless and repetitive forms. They show less sensitivity to the form or tactility of an object than to its frequency and availability (or lack of it). Collections are a manifestation of the same American temperament that sees growth, progress, aggrandizement, and expansion as good things in themselves, that sees any registration of quantity as admirable.

The term *conversation piece* has been used to designate objects which serve no purposes, or have outgrown them, and are now only good to be looked at, scrutinized, and discussed when the parties present are sufficiently dull to leave no other topic of conversation. These objects are usually placed on the coffee table in the room to which the guests will retire after their dinner. Although conversation pieces may take any form, they are such that eventually a guest, more sensitive than the others to the burden of awkward silences, will suddenly point to the object, saying, "My, my, isn't that an interesting little thing! You must explain to all of us, Catherine, what that is!" At this point, a story is related, or perhaps manufactured on the spot, tracing the object's origin to an island that someone present has happened to visit. Soon everyone is talking excitedly about this tropical haven, and the conversation piece has revealed its nature to be essentially functional.

The conversation piece is an object so peculiar or anachronistic that no function can be assigned to it. Yet, somehow it is too "pretty" to discard. Closely related to it is the keepsake, which is a useless object that is thrown away but quickly retrieved by teary aunts and little girls who stow it away in their dresser drawers to pet on rainy days. In both cases, however, only pretenses are made to treat the object as an aesthetic particular. If its value isn't functional, it's nostalgic. Furthermore, conversation pieces are taken only from among those objects which have no function. They take on a nonfunctional aspect only because they have outgrown functions. A true sensitivity to objects sees, on the other hand, that objects with a definite and valuable function *also* possess unique aesthetic lives of their own.

A third example of objects in a nonfunctional context is Pop Art, in which advertising emblems, promotional displays, etc., are treated by the artist not as functional vehicles, but as decorative cultural facts. Actually, the process that Pop Art puts a capitalist tool like the Coca-Cola sign through is the process which we should instinctively put all objects we observe. The exaggerated way in which the pop artist isolates the object and inserts it into a relatively unconnotative environment, such as a museum, where it demands to be judged as a self-sufficient phenomenon is the way in which we should begin to understand the thousands of objects which people our lives. Although achieving a sensitivity to all objects is not Pop Art's ultimate goal, we can learn from its motives.

3.

Sengle had taken it for granted that, owing to his proven influence on the behaviour of small objects, he had a right to assume that the whole world would, in all likelihood, obey him.

— Alfred Jarry, *Les Jours et Les Nuits*

This, unfortunately, is an assumption too many of us make. We have come to believe that "thaw and open" is a dictate that, if followed, will bring the universe under our control. We don't see that function is a virtue of technology, not of our lives. "The world, ultimately, is an aesthetic phenomenon —that is to say, the world (all there is) cannot, ultimately, be justified." (Susan Sontag, *Against Interpretation*.) Because we have grown to think that the world and its objects are really at our service, rather than thinking that the world is a gift that our senses equip us to appreciate, long walks and quiet sittings are things which have fallen out of favor, things which have even become embarrassing to suggest, things which for many have become real impossibilities.

There are many people who ride buses back and forth because buses touch them in a way nothing else can; I know people who carry objects in their pockets to feel and study from time to time. Yet most of the people in my neighborhood are noted for their dispassionate relationships with objects. It is time to think about cultivating a sense of non-affluent materialism. Not possessing things, not wanting things, just being aware of and being able to judge the physical world.

The fact that the world is flooded with so many objects is clearly not good in itself; it merely happens to be a fact of our existence. Our task becomes one of feeling as many as we can, sorting them out, of placing the ones we like closest to us and the many we find offensive as far away from us as we can.

(Living too much inside of ourselves, inside of the poems we read, too much inside of the houses we inhabit, too much inside of our intellects, we can no longer sense the textures and surfaces and forms of the world. Crawling inside of ourselves, we have locked ourselves out of our own aesthetic sense.)

Take *thing*. Like all words, *thing* is an object which assumes its own aural form, weight, color, and brilliance. It is rounded at one end and tapered at the other like a top or, better, like one of those large pipettes with the rubber bulb at the end used to spray water on raging fires in the outdoor grill. *Thing* is water poured from a height of three feet into a saucer on the floor; it is panty hose.

This notion that a word can be interpreted in so many ways just reinforces the knowledge that there are too many things in the world. Here are some of them:

dogs	taps
legs	tips
spigots	pits
faucets	tremors
robinets	capons

capers

antihistamines

preserved eggs

books

leeks

traits

Noxzema

tuna

emphysema

Cleveland

tooth powder

weavings

lathes

shavings

chowder

mantises

oaks

wherries

Waring blenders

dental floss

barlow knives

woks

alderman

batter

borders

Durkee's dressing

encomiums

abscesses

abacuses

elbow macaroni

nozzles

nubbins

Lugers

bobbins

nostrums

rashes

rashers

saucers

sorghum

and

chilled gutted fish

Which of these objects is the largest?

Which is the smallest?

What are the differences between them?

Which have you used?

Which ones are absolutely necessary?

Which may be replaced by objects with which we are more familiar?

Which of these objects are the most articulate?

The least?

Which objects are described by words which sound like their shape?

Which sound like their use?

Do any of these objects have a use?

For which of these objects did we develop a use?

This should be convincing proof that there are too many objects. But considering this proliferation, particularly of brands, of the synonymous article, we must be prepared to distinguish among them, to eliminate superfluous choices, to discern between Whopper Burgers and Big Macs.

It is not a question of moving objects into the areas of the exotic or the mundane. A critical gesture of that sort can confuse identities. We should simply *sense* the formation of categories; to visualize relationships and distinctions tacitly makes it in the end unnecessary to construct our formal, specious categories.

Try this exercise. Collect as many of the objects in the above list as you can. In the event your favorite articles are not included, you may want to locate them. You should also get any object not included in the list which appeals to you. Gather all the objects when you are done into the largest, most vacant room available; a living room, a garage, a gymnasium. Placing yourself as close to the center of the floor as you can, arrange the objects around you, putting those you love closest to you, those you like least against the walls. Do not let an object's function interfere in the least with your placement procedures. You may need your toilet, but if you truly dislike it, it must go against the walls like any other undesirable object. This is how your universe of objects is aesthetically arranged, how you find your place in the order of things.

But remember to create spaces around the objects, don't crowd them, let them breathe.

4. More quotes:

Where the Romantics made nature the object of their radical aesthetic politics and the freedom to respond—to nightingale, skylark, daffodils and the rest—seem like a revolutionary principle, the Moderns [American and English poets] seem utterly unaware of their world outside. They live in and on internal landscapes which they may or may not project onto the outer world as seems convenient . . . . The outer world only seems to exist inasmuch as it can be used.
        —A. Alvarez, *Under Pressure*

The world exists, not for what it means but for what it is. The purpose of mushrooms is to be mushrooms; wine is in order

to be wine: Things are precious before they are contributory.
      —Father Robert Capon, *The Supper of the Lamb*

Even now, after these few pages on objects, I sense my hypocrisy. If I were really sensitive to objects, I wouldn't talk
about them at such length. I have tried to stop myself from
interferring with the lives of objects, from acting as their
biographer, yet those few pages constitute no less an affront to,
no less an intrusion in, their affairs. Having only translated
my actual violations into a verbal one, my apparent concern
for my subject matter allows me to get away with it. But am I
really concerned? I have not only been unable to keep my
hands off, but I have been unable to keep my words off. I will
not permit the objects to flow toward me, to fill my world
with themselves. I force them to merge with my life instead
of acknowledging their proper places. I lunge at them, flitting
from the toaster to the faucet, setting my alarm clock; I prance
about arranging erasers and paper clips, setting a book flush
against the edge of the table; I pry open a bottle. The room
recoils at my touch. Someone passes me a plate of appetizers.
Without looking to see what they are, I attack one, filling my
mouth with its unnameable textures. I turn on the radio,
spinning the channel selector back and forth, demanding only
music. I have no idea what is inside my Zenith Royal 810 and
don't care; give me music. And now I write about these ob-
objects, spinning words around them, weaving arguments
through them, clogging their gears with polemics, flooding
their motors with explanations, stunting their growth with
pithy maxims. I violate the canapé. I give them names without knowing if they are the right names. In my list, I included
tooth powder, but how can I be sure I wasn't thinking of
curry powder or bath talc?

> Human beings are so "fallen" that they must start with the
> simplest linguistic act: The naming of things. Perhaps no
> more than this minimal function can be preserved from the
> general corruption of discourse . . . A tremendous spiritual

preparation . . . is required for this deceptively simple act of naming. It is nothing less than the scouring and harmonious sharpening of the senses.

— Susan Sontag, *Styles of Radical Will*

Just as persons whose names we know are honored with attentions we withhold from anonymity, objects we can identify, are familiar with, receive the consideration they deserve. Let's get out and start naming! Point to objects and try to associate the name and the thing in the same way we began to memorize, on the first day of third grade, the names of new students in our class. The act of specifying, of naming correctly, of distinguishing between cloud formations, between kinds of fish, between colors, between emotions, dignifies our relationships by restoring an understanding of singularities.

The person who slips behind the luncheon counter and yells, "Give me some food!" or who enters a haberdashery and announces, "I want some clothes" is not capable of interpreting the physical world he lives in nor is he particularly attentive to his senses. This same impulse to crowd all the members of a genus namelessly under one roof creates, when carried to logical extents, wars in which genocide becomes more possible than ever before because the government has thought and taught its nation to think of the South East Asians only in terms of inimical statistics. It is the impulse that makes it possible to violate spheres which don't belong to us—natural resources, foreign countries, our own cities, Black Panther headquarters, each other's life. Agnew's infamous comment that if you've seen one ghetto, you've seen them all betrays more than just the inveterate stupidity we take for granted; it betrays the inexcusable mode of thinking in generalities which not only does harm to individuals, but kills them with napalm, nerve gas, and hunger.

I remember, vaguely, a scene in an old movie about the Civil War. A Yankee soldier leaves his campsite at night to get a drink at a stream. As he stoops at the water, he realizes he is next to a Confederate soldier who has come also to drink and be in the darkness. Disarmed by the meeting, they exchange a few words about the night or the war, and then, bayonets still affixed to their muskets, they part and trod back noiselessly to their respective camps. Impressed with his own particularity in that moment, neither soldier could threaten that of another which he saw so clearly.

Peace is the moment in which we ascribe life to everything around us.

The Story of Baseball

That evens the count at two and two.

—Jack Brickhouse

This is how our lives began. Out of our neighbors' radios;
they cried at the crucial moments, leaping out of their barbecue pits. Even on those cool and sunny days when we wished
to read quietly in our patios, we couldn't keep the go-ahead
run out of our lives. Baseball seeped out of hot darkened windows on the South Side. Men could be imagined in those
tenement rooms, adjusting the radio with movements of their
index fingers. Mothers and their tiny sons waddled onto the
El platform after the game, their ears still pressed to the tran-
sistor to hear the totals. In our own living rooms, the TV was
on. It was the fifth inning of a game in late June between two
clubs who had already long ago forfeited their chances for first
place; like old men playing checkers in the park, they would
play out their insignificant wins and losses with no hope of
final victory. What about the '51 Giants, someone in the
room says. But it is universally understood, it is the consensus
of all the probabilities, that this year, with this schedule, that
will not happen; there will be no '51 Giants, just the long un-

wavering decrescendo that hits, sometime early in October, the end of the season.

But that makes no difference. Everyone is absorbed by the image on the screen, lost in the sanctity of the moment. Two and Two Two on Two out, the pitcher is looking in, curling his upper lip as he tries to read the catcher. The close-up lens on the TV camera takes us right up to his face, takes us right up to the critical microsecond, to his moist brow. We, in the living room, react tremendously to the way he fingers the ball in the glove, as if he had just done the impossible, as if he had just opened walnuts with his teeth. The pitcher is still looking in, his hands on his knees. There is some misunderstanding, and the catcher trots out and puts his arm around the pitcher. They stand together on the mound for a while, their lean shadows pointing toward right field. Behind their heads, faces in the left-center field bleachers bob up and down, red with sun. The catcher trots back to home plate. No one in the room has looked up. The pitcher sets, looks sensually over his shoulder at the runners. The whole room devotes its attention to this moment. Even the dog on the floor convinces us, with an anthropomorphic gesture, that he too is watching, and understanding this moment. All of baseball is focused on this instant; the meaning of the game has fallen on this pitcher's shoulders. Outside the window, nothing moves. It is Sunday, June 28, and the whole nation hangs on this pitch.

It is a strike.

The pitcher, as if he knew ten minutes ago that it would be a strike, is already halfway to the dugout, head down; he understands the weight of his small triumph. He is the student returning from the blackboard, having correctly added the row of numbers. In the living room, we all relax, fall back in our chairs. The pitcher belongs to our team. It is our team which has benefitted. We're going into the bottom of the fifth and there isn't one person in the room who doesn't know that the third baseman is going to lead off.

2. Often we went to games. It's night baseball. The grass is luminously green, the ball absolutely white; from a distance it looks like a Canada mint. All the colors fulfilling their potential; and the players are so fine in their uniforms, so clear and thick thighed and well shaven. They seem so otherworldly in the light of the small day created by the light towers, so tall and chrome. It is as if they are charged with a current and would burn our fingers if we touched them. We all want a victory, and we all want to find our seats, and we all want programs, but no desire at the moment surpasses that of wanting to touch the baseball players.

When I was eleven and had a passion for first basemen's gloves, my father and I went to a night game. When I saw Earl Torgeson on the field with his first baseman's glove playing catch casually with Jim Landis, I had a desire to put his glove on, to put a major league first baseman's glove on my hand. I told my father to tell Earl Torgeson to come on over by the dugout where we were standing. My father smiled because he thought I wanted to meet Earl Torgeson. That wasn't the case since Earl hardly ever played. This wasn't like the time I met Bobby Hull, *Bobby Hull*, over the glass at the side of the rink before a game with the Detroit Red Wings. I can talk about that the way an uncle of mine talks about the time he photographed Patton pissing in the Rhine, front view. Earl Torgeson isn't even like the time Bill Monbouquette no-hit the White Sox on August 1, 1962, and I almost touched him over the roof of the dugout as he made his way in a crowd of teammates to the locker room. He was the enemy and I didn't even actually touch him, but it was still more than Earl Torgeson. All I really want to do is to touch his glove and be close to the leather, to put the big leather over my little hand. Come on over, my father called out to Earl, I got my son here and he wants to meet you. It might have been the first time any fan wanted Earl to come over, so he dropped what he was doing and hustled up to the wall and leaned over. Then he said, as he had probably heard a regular say, Hiya Kid. Hi Earl, I said, and left it at that. Uh, Earl, my father broke in quickly, my son here wants to know if he can try on your mitt for a minute. Yeah, I said, lemme try on your glove, Big Earl. Earl took off his mitt and slipped it on my hand. It was warm from his hand, moist from the sweat. It was soft and soft brown. It was mystical. It was like the first time you feel yourself inside a woman.

The infield dirt is intense brown, smoothed over by the gray-and-crimson-uniformed ground crew. The white lime foul-lines are perfectly straight, the bases clean, ivory, the outfield fences so definitive; high and light green in left and center, low and light green in right; the bull pens clearly demarcated by the right-field wall. The beautiful combination of outfield fence distances; we think of all those we have known: 379, 411, 365, 340, 380, 366, 391, 461! We wish they had painted the distances on the walls every five feet so we could trace the wonderful movement from 340 down the line to 410 in center. Dead center!

Foul territory distinguished from fair by the most fastidiously straight lines. Here is the batter's box. Perfect. Two bulky rectangles straddling the plate; the batter will know exactly where to stand. And the plate itself is also white, so white and understandable it can be seen from the most obscure seat in the bleachers. Above the bleachers, the sky is navy blue, suffused with the glow of the lights and the neon signs on adjacent buildings. The sky rises and it blackens as it rises, until it's perfectly black overhead. Below, the stadium is lit and white, an illuminated corner of the universe.

The boundaries are so obvious and the rules so clear. It is a world without question; even the belligerent ball players have learned that their disputes with the umpires are purely a formality, a picturesque disobedience, hardly an affront to the issues of balls and strikes and the utter certitude of the light green scoreboard in center field. In fact, everyone is afraid that the game will end too soon, this game of yes and no, win

and loss, hoorah and harangue, and we will all be pushed out
of the gates back into the world where no one keeps track of
our RBIs.

So here in the left-field-line grandstands, we are all shouting
and eating and hoping neither rain nor boredom will put an
end to the game. Look at that field! It's so green, and all the
players have taken their positions, knowing exactly where to
go and stand and wait for the ball to be hit to them, for their
tiny round messiah to come and free them from the ennui of
ennuis, major league baseball. For baseball is essentially the
imperturable grace of the players waiting in their positions.
One chews gum and thinks of his children. One paws at the
dirt in the same way after every pitch; one recites to himself
the suggested field positions to defense each hitter in the opposing batting order. But all are occupied, crouched and eager,
by being precisely what they are, major league baseball players.

Here in the stands we are occupied, more and less, by the
demands of our tentative profession, that of being fans in the
left-field stands. We come from all over. Many of the fans
know each other and pound each other on the back and the
head. There is a young Italian whose nose and chin, should
they continue to grow as they have, will touch in a few more
seasons. He laughs and hoots at the row of old men behind
him, hitting one with his program. The old man returns the
good-natured gesture. "What the shit!" he says. "What the
shit?"

"Hey!" the young guy says, "What the shit?"

"Oh, yeah?" the old man says, "What the fuck!"

"What the shit, what the fuck!" the guy says. "You can't
even get yours up anymore!" and the original good humor is
lost in rising anger.

"Hell," the old man says, "I've been using a heavier bat
than you for fifty years!!"

"Hey old man," the guy says, "you better watch your shit."

"Wanna a fuckin' fist in your face?" a friend of the old man
says.

"You couldn't hurt a bat boy, four eyes," the guy says. "Just watch it, old man."

"You little shit," the old man says, "you fuckin' better watch it."

"Just shut the fuck up."

"Yeah," says another guy, "everybody shut the fuck up! Bobby's at the plate."

"Yeah," says the guy, "shut the fuck up. Look who's up."

"Fuck it," says the old man. "Look who's up."

3. Some of us even got on the field ourselves. We sold our bodies and minds to baseball coaches for the summer in return for the occasional applause of local parents and an explosion of the baseball myth. Before our eyes, baseball was demystified. We made backhanded grabs worthy of the major leagues, running catches that defied our age and experience. Emissaries from the big leagues followed the stars on our teams to distant prairie towns where they threw their arms around them after the game. Baseball, a realm that two years before had seemed untouchable, defined by dimensions larger than our own, was reduced to its proper size. The last game of my high school career was umpired by a man who, a few years earlier, had played first base for the Chicago Cubs. Since that time, he had succumbed to vices incompatible with the game, felt his mortality a bit too poignantly, and was finally booked for running naked through the streets of the city. Now, unable to do better than a high school umpiring job, he accepted his lot quietly without integrity, missing close calls here and there. Once intolerably removed from the game we loved, we had gotten too close. We saw that this man's future involved a fate so low we had never considered it for ourselves. Once a star, he now served us. His demise was ours.

When we went back, as we now did less frequently, to a major league ball game, we sat in the bleachers in right. We noticed the pitchers waiting in the bull pen for the game to end. They were too old to be dressed up in red and white uniforms. They seemed to have the faces of bankers, designers, electricians, but not baseball players. They warmed up until they were finally told to sit down, the rally had been quelled, they would not be needed. They hung their chins over the Cyclone fence in right, anticipating the last out. We anticipated the entire game and would leave the game in the fifth, feeling odd. Later, we would learn about the reserve clause, would sense what it was like to be traded from one city to another without being consulted. In high school, if we were cut, we returned to our home or the classroom. These men moved their lives to San Diego or Cincinnati. We learned that the absurd power structure that governed in high school was in control everywhere. The inequity we thought endemic only to secondary education was revealed to us to be the order mistaken by the entire world for justice.

Once baseball had been so ubiquitous it was thought to be a habit indispensable to national health. Now, it seemed so peculiar as a thing to be taken seriously that we wondered for an instant how we could have played it like we did. Coming to our senses, we remembered that, living as we did, we had had no choice.

But the passion for baseball did not die overnight; in fact, a faint scar will always remain. In an effort to revive dying interest, we sought to enhance the game in a number of ways. When we learned that baseball had very little substance, that it consisted of a random order of rehearsed plays, we compensated by perfecting the form of each motion, of stylizing every gesture. What we spent most of the games doing, standing around, became an art. Our models were major leaguers and we would observe the nuances of their play. During infield practice before the game, we cocked our heads at special angles, sensuously rolled our gum between our lips and teeth. We pulled our socks tautly over our calves. We affected an exaggerated style of throwing which drew attention to our coordination and physique. Since the game itself was so underplayed, so devoid of inherent excitement, personal mannerism had to be overplayed as much as possible. At moments during the game that were not even crucial, I would strut to the mound from my position at first base. The scattered fans would interpret this as important strategy. I would say to the pitcher that I had had no reason to come to the mound, that it merely seemed like a good, dramatic thing to do. Most of the time, the pitcher would scoff at me, spitting furiously, which was, in itself, superbly histrionic.

I felt deeply that there was a rhythm, a decor, that had to be preserved. I don't know if many of my teammates were really aware to what extent they padded the sport with style. Didn't they see that the pace of baseball was so slow there was no hope of losing oneself in the action? We *had* to superimpose an emotional structure that wasn't part of the game itself. We stepped out of the batter's box after a pitch to adjust our helmets, our pants, to rub the bridge of our nose; overreacted to pitches, devising pained expressions that impressed the fans.

There was no body contact, so we manufactured it. We touched each other compulsively on the bench; we pretended it was an active game by running to our positions at the beginning of each inning and running off at the end. (In other sports, the participants are too tired to run handsomely to the locker room.) To me, it became a game whose only meaning was that which I had decided to ascribe to it.

Another way we learned to dignify baseball was this: Whether playing or watching it, we began to use an outrageously sophisticated vocabulary to describe the game. We talked intently of psychology, character, motives, trends, aggressions. No outfielder simply caught the ball for an out. He drifted back, shielding his eyes from the sun, faded toward right center, felt behind him for the fence, looked for an instant at the runner over at third, braced himself, squinted, pulled it in. What was a simple act, performed a hundred times during the season, thousands during practice, became the object of calculated description.

(This habit of overextending our verbal and intellectual

powers became a popular, if not a healthy, habit. The banalities of our lives in college, for instance, were transformed into the complexities of merely existing. We sucked everything dry of its poetry and subtlety, a walk at night, the discovery of a new author, a reflection on a friend. Scenes which should have filled us with what they merely were sent us rhapsodizing. "This reminds me of Röskilke when the sun dropped behind the houses." Our reactions drew attention to themselves and not to their stimulis. Maybe we thought we could homogenize the universe with words. A bum in the darkened bleachers became the archetype of human suffering.)

The terms and jargon of baseball assumed for us a metaphorical quality. It went further than junior high school when we spoke of advancing sexually zone to zone as one advances from base to base:

> So he blazed away for her with his golden bat. It was not really golden, it was white, but in the sun it sometimes flashed gold and some of the opposing pitchers complained it shone in their eyes.
>
> —Bernard Malamud, *The Natural*

> His raincoat had a slit in the lining behind his pocket, and this she reached through to slip her hand into his coin pocket. . . . She was trying to get her other hand on the bat, gal can't take a healthy swing without a decent grip, after all, but she couldn't get both hands through the slit.
>
> —Robert Coover, *The Universal Baseball Association, J. Henry Waugh, prop.*

As we internalized the rhythm of the game, we found its elements everywhere. From time to time, everyone had a three and two count on him, everyone was sent to the showers, everyone was trying to stretch it into a double, everyone was on his way up from the minor leagues, everyone was taken out of the play or had a broken bat. We absorbed the radio announcer's speech pattern as if it were a tape recording played to us nightly as we slept.

4.

Because writing about sports is the sole literary expression of
the sports reporter, he brings to bear on this single limited out-
let the repressed emotions from a dozen other areas. Under
his hand, games and the grown-up boys and girls who play
them for money in this country become magnified into a picture of life itself. Readers are often made to feel the same
heartfelt emotions toward the athletes that used to be reserved for a wife, a close friend, or the victims of a mine
cave-in. . . .
                    —Seymour Krim, *Views of a Near-Sighted Cannoneer*

Without heroes we're all plain people and don't know how
far we can go.
    You mean the big guys set the records and the little bug-
gers try and bust them?
                    —Bernard Malamud, *The Natural*

5. If football or stock car racing is the cultural symbol of the
American as carnivore, baseball is the symbol of American
as silent majoritarian. First, baseball is entirely *understood*.
Not just the conclusion to each play, but also its dynamics and
the simple psychology that the game parades as intricacy.
Everyone *knows* why the manager is bringing in a lefty to face
the left-handed batter. Who here doesn't know why the short-
stop threw to first instead of second on that ground ball? Or
why he should have thrown to first? Everyone knows why the
center fielder caught the ball instead of letting it drop in front
of him.
    Baseball is a game which, freed from the exigencies of a
time limit, proceeds at a leisurely rate it has determined for
itself. In most other competitive team sports, the clarity of
each act, each motion, each decision is lost in the density of
play. The other sports, involving more contact, replace baseball's man–ball confrontation with man–man confrontations,
but more importantly replace isolated man–ball confrontations with rapidly successive and simultaneous man–man

confrontations. In baseball, all eyes are now on the batter. He has a full count on him and the friction between him and the pitcher is the only thing really happening on the ball field. While the pitcher fidgets on the mound, the fans in the stands are already calculating the possible outcomes of the pitch, the situations that might result or might be eliminated. In football, each single play generates multiple confrontations, all occurring at once, all bearing on the success of the play. Every spectator, selecting one confrontation to focus on, necessarily misses all the others. Although he may have watched the quarterback on that play and followed the ball, he has not seen the subtler clashes, he has missed the overall dynamics. He claims he has seen the play, but in fact he has only seen a glimpse of it. The spectator must acknowledge the selectivity which is involved in observing games like football, basketball, and hockey. These are games which, to a large extent, are outside the visual, even the theoretical control of the spectator. They concern a complexity beyond the power of the fan to understand it fully at the moment. But the logic of baseball is more linear.

That each action in baseball, a walk to the mound, a double, a slider, is isolated from the general flow of the game in both time and space, is not the primary example of baseball's simplicity. In baseball, the contingencies of each act are few and repetitive. So much so, in fact, that every baseball coach is able to inform his players what to do in virtually every conceivable situation before he even takes to the field. Baseball involves the joy of seeing the same fundamental motion successfully completed again and again. (Here, pitchers must be exempted.) Take a play: a ground ball to the second baseman. Each grounder is distinguished from the next by the slightest vicissitudes; height of hop, speed, direction. And the second baseman has foreseen all the potential of the ground ball to him. There is nothing that he doesn't expect from it. He may have to dive to stop it, but he has foreseen that possibility. He knows the ball will not suddenly fake to its right and dart out to left field. He knows the ball will not come to a stop a tantalizing few feet in front of him, then shoot through his legs as he stoops to pick it up. He knows he is not dealing with another person who, at any minute, might choose to display his human ability to deceive or surprise. In most cases, the second baseman will move appropriately and field the ball, aware of certain principles of motion, and throw to first. The first baseman, barring the infrequent bad throw, will catch the ball, confident that it will not try to elude his glove. After this play, the crowd, who has expected nothing less than the perfect execution of the 4–3 put-out, still applauds, at times almost as if the impossible had been performed.

It is possible to say that the applause isn't for the excellence of the play itself, but for the simple fact of the out. The ball club is now one out closer to victory or defeat. That is what one applauds.

Yet it can't be denied that a great part of the applause goes out to those players for the play they have just made. In other sports, say, hockey, applause seems well deserved. If a wing makes a good move, eludes a defenseman, and brings the puck over the blue line, he merits applause even if he doesn't score. His feat is far more formidable than the outfielder's catch. He has not only successfully controlled the puck, but he has outwitted the opposition, that is, men as capable of deception, aggression, and interference as he. One becomes an accomplished hockey player only when he achieves the ability to react correctly in an instantaneous situation that he has never seen before. The hockey player has the puck at a certain moment, and at that moment, the other eleven players on the ice have arranged themselves in a certain pattern; it is a condition that has never been duplicated.

In baseball, one becomes proficient at fielding a hopper at second and making the throw to first in the way one becomes adept at backing the car out of the driveway. In the end, probably, what does make mystical the 4–3 put-out is the awareness of a fact that is both taken for granted and lost in the rapid pace of other sports: The fact that the accumulation of successful 4–3 put-outs and other retirements of opposing batters leads, eventually, to larger successes. Each putout smells faintly to the fans of an ascension in the standings. In other sports, of course, the success of individual maneuvers is contributive to the success of the team and so on, but those simple associations are lost in the intensity of play. In baseball, each fan can recline after every out and say to himself, five outs to a victory, and if we win this one we go three up on the Phils and are one behind the Pirates. In baseball, the interludes allow the spectator complete freedom of thought; he is almost able to study the game at the same time he watches it.

So, with the exception of an unbelievable catch or a clutch home run, the bulk of any baseball game consists of widely spaced moments of no inherent brilliance. These moments are interesting only in relation to the vacuity of the surrounding silences. The batted ball, the white pill drifting toward the glove, sailing across the faces of the fans in the lower deck, the foul ball animating a whole section of the grandstands, the sight of a favorite ballplayer's head in the dugout—everything that takes place is exciting because it saves us from the game's ultimate tedium. Spectators waiting endless, intolerable innings for a hit, a modest play, a recollection of what baseball must be like, like prison inmates waiting in their cells for a meal, to be let out, anything at all, happy even to see the guard pass.

6. Connotatively speaking, this is partly why baseball is a sport of the silent majoritarians. It is a slow, uneventful review of existence; it serves to reinforce the dull second to first of the lives of those who never tried for an extra base. It is a game in which man opposes an object, not other human beings. It is a game in which the players do not have to assert themselves on defense. Generally, the ball comes to them. They experience the offensive only four or five times a game. The spectators are not consumed by the action; neither are

they left behind. One goes to get a hot dog. The game continues. One discerns immediately what occurred in his absence. If other sports are like elegant meals with numerous dishes, conversations, and drinks, in which the guests finally tire themselves out with their own activity, baseball is an outdoor barbecue, equipped with Briquettes, ribs, slaw, and soda.

There are other reasons why baseball seems to characterize distinctly middle-class American tendencies. Baseball, more so than other sports, is a game of individual endeavor. The illusion that it is a team sport comes solely from the fact that it is played by a team. On the field, the players do not all move together; in fact, many do not move at all. Fluidity is confined to only a few members of the team who react while the others are not required to. In reality, even a double play is the automatic response of two or three individuals to a familiar situation. It is important to remember that although baseball is essentially an individual sport, the individuals perform within a highly routinized structure. Baseball attempts to convince its fans that each play is an individual act when, in most cases, it is an individual reaction.

Baseball is the game of the great hitter at the plate, all by himself, doing something for the team, yet acting on his own. But baseball is Jacksonian democracy in a more crucial way. It is a game for all classes, but particularly for the lower classes. Football is the game of college graduates and ostentatious publicity. Baseball is the game of nineteen-year-old toughs off the street. It is the game of the man who emerges from obscurity long enough for a few clutch hits, an all-star appearance, and a few endorsements before he is returned to the anonymous populace. It is a game for the small, even the uncoordinated; strength is not very important . . .

Another salient fact of baseball which tends to level differences democratically is the element of chance in hitting. With rare exceptions, batters have very little control over where they hit the ball. The control they assert is only over whether they hit the ball at all or not. Once a ball is hit, its chances of falling safely are not determined by variables that might logically be assumed to have importance: force and distance. Long balls are caught for outs four hundred feet from the plate, while accidental hits fall for doubles one hundred thirty feet down the line. One player hits a line drive that is caught. Another bounces a ball ("That ball had eyes.") through the middle for a single. Only in the case of a home run is a hitter's effort quickly rewarded by payment in the game's currency, runs. But two feet this side of a home run is an out. And, of course, two feet this side of the President of the United States is a janitor or used car salesman.

In the long view, the better hitters rise to the top; percentages finally unveil their greatness. But on a smaller scale, players are rewarded for providential favor ("Well, Lloyd, they just seem to be falling in there this season.") as often as they are for prowess, ability.

7.

(UPI) The Atlanta Braves unveiled today a computer they hope will eventually provide more statistics for baseball.

By punching several specially coded keys, the Braves will be able to know in a matter of seconds not only batting averages or pitching records, but also how a performer did in a variety of clutch situations. One item the computer turned up immediately in a demonstration was that, although Clete Boyer is barely hitting above .200 he has one of the best averages on the team for driving home runners from second or third. . . .

"Statistics are one of baseball's strongest traditions," said Lee Walburn, Braves' public relations director. . . .

—*The New York Times*

Baseball became the nation's favorite game during a violent, squalid industrialization. . . . Baseball was not only an escape; it reinforced capitalist values. The game treated people as property. "Trading" and "bonuses" were a means of improving efficiency and sharpening competition. Baseball also incorporated "stealing"—a risk proportional to an individual's ability and his luck. Industry increased production

through standardization; so did baseball. Batting averages,
earned-run averages were comfortable percentiles, simple cal-
culations in a world of outrageous figures and complicated
equations. . . .

—John Lahr, "The Theatre of Sports"
Evergreen November, 1969

Baseball, because it is so comprehensible, so stylistically
unambiguous, gives its viewers a sense of control over the
game that other sports, which hinge on decisions we are rarely
equipped to understand or make, deprive us of. Baseball gives
the spectator what is so dearly lacking in his life—a sense of
being the manipulator, the employer. *Everyone is the manager.* By being broken down into moments of clear-cut dualism
(out–safe, strike–ball, etc.), baseball often grants the avid fan
a fifty–fifty chance of accurately predicting any outcome.
This is more of a bargain than hockey, for example, whose
action, again, is too rapid and complex to admit prognosis.

As far as spectators are concerned, ballplayers live their
entire lives on the field. It may be heard that the wife of one
has just given birth to a new boy, that another has opened a
carry-out chicken franchise, but their existence only has
meaning for them when they appear, in their clean uniforms,
at their positions on the field. It is as if the fan in the stand
believes that a certain player finds himself in left field at this
point in his life only for the fan's benefit.

8. So often lately we have been noticed in the mezzanines.
Is it just that baseball is a spectacle, a colorful ritual? That its
pace allows us to sensitize ourselves to the whole environment,
to observe changes in the sky, the posture of other fans? Do
we go for the game itself, for Public Association, to get out
side, to get outside of ourselves?

The moment is for us; we witness its prolonged suspense.
And when the suspense builds up, when the rally is mounted,
when the action seems to pursue its climax but when nothing
happens, the batter goes down looking with the bags full,

how can we really be disappointed? Baseball teaches us that this is the way things turn out.

Mostly, there is something so excruciatingly deliberate, so studied, so manifestly dull, so reminiscent of our own lives in the game that we are drawn to it for its reflections of what we know. There are times when we savor, when we cheer for rain delays, pray for postponements of the action, pray perversely for long ball games studded with full counts and walks to the mound, pray for our own lethargy. Suppose we watch the first two innings on TV and turn it off. When we return it is the bottom of the eighth, and we haven't missed any of the action. There is no action to miss.

Baseball is the sport which excuses our own lassitude.

Baseball is not liked; it is well liked. And it is a bad game, a very bad game. But we go back again and again to see ourselves in action.

Watching the Descent
from a Folding Chair

1. My parents were married in 1941. In the grainy black-and-white silent film of their lavish wedding, my aunts, my uncles, my grandparents, long lost friends, dance in large revolving circles. They almost look like another breed; the women's calves seem too thick, the men too short, the gestures too premeditated and public. Now the photographer fixes them at the buffet table, petits fours and finger sandwiches suspended in front of their mouths. The print has faded. As my mother walks up the aisle, her face explodes in a patch of light. My grandfather's eyes are indistinct, lost in charcoal shadows. In the background, others are featureless altogether. They do not possess any distinguishing characteristics, only gray forms that suggest complete faces and bodies. When they move toward the camera, they evolve identities; my heritage materializes. My parents, in the room watching the movie, call out a name. It is a friend they have rarely seen since. His eyes cannot avoid the photographer, and he smiles wanly in our direction, groping for an expression. I am positive he has something to do with my life. He is the man with a name like Sy or Sam or Harold who is known to me only as the tiny wizened gentleman who appears at the house now and then for family affairs. Next there is a couple at the buffet

table. She smiles broadly at the camera, exposing radiant white teeth between two strenuous strokes of almost black lipstick. He, on the other hand, is looking only at her, puckering his lips, intent on recording his buss for posterity. She refuses to acknowledge him at first, but when it becomes clear that the photographer will not leave until he has his kiss, she spins around to face him and then they meet, close-mouthed, joyously. In a second, they are both facing the camera again with their impervious grins. There, wheeling in front of the camera during a rumba, my aunt's face passes. She is in her thirties, a very successful photographer with a stage name, living in Los Angeles. I imagine that she is impeccably dressed and made up, but the quality of the print keeps me from these details. If anything, she seems proud. Now, in her sixties, she prowls her pungent apartment on the West coast, sunk in stuffy memories, leafing through yellow prints depicting opening nights and exhibitions she once covered.

Both my grandfathers are handsome. My father's father, stout and bald already, but with clear eyes and impressively aquiline nose, glides down the aisle with grandma who nods sunnily to her left and right, coquettishly provoking the comments her matronly beauty deserves. When she was twelve and working in a dry goods store in Warsaw, my grandfather, then eighteen, fell in love and waited six years outside the window for her. I don't know very much about their marriage, except that there were serious quarrels as there always are, a separation; there was a genuine concern for culture on her side, a sturdy Calvinism on his. Consequently, they were neither artistic nor prosperous beyond hardship. Education did not play much of a role in their life, but beauty and practical learning did; similarly, money wasn't everything, but it was how life got better. Their grandsons were destined to become both businessmen and artists. Religion was the real world; it was what made everything possible. My grandfather prayed twice a day, everyday, until he died, wrapping the

tefillin around his forearm. Long after he had lost his power
of speech on his deathbed, a nurse came in one morning and
found him staring up, his lips moving rapidly and silently.

The photographer is once again at the buffet. There are
interminable shots of guests eating, smiling with their mouths
full; the camera lingers, making painful accusations; its victims
look away and swallow hard. Then they are all dancing again.
My mother's father, thin and slightly balding, is a striking
figure. Shorter than my mother, whom he escorts down the
aisle at the beginning of the movie, he still exudes a grandeur
that the act of living has since taken from him. He is someone
who would buy you a drink. The last three decades have not
asked anything extraordinary from him, but the common
stresses of the years have made their changes. He has observed
his children and grandchildren growing, caught them in the
act of becoming what he once was; his business has gotten
better, but more frequently worse. He has been a victim of
unrewarded generosity, a major operation, and clearly defined
images of death. It was no longer thought of as a philosophical
matter, but rather as something that might occur the next
day, like a thunderstorm or an improvement in the fur business. Thirty years after the wedding, he would walk into the
room and complain about stomach pains and the possible
reemergence of a tumor. It was not so much that he had a
stomach ache; it had more to do with an impatience with
life, yet a longing for it, an intimation of the end, an understanding of the cycle of human seasons.

For his wife, my Nanny, the direction of life was more
easily seen. In the movie, she is beautiful and black-haired,
with broad shoulders. Dancing with grandpa, she wears a
charming and careful smile. In seventeen years, she will be
paralyzed on her right side, the victim of a stroke. For the
next twelve, she lives as an invalid but, finding strengths she
never knew were within her, eventually learns to walk using
only a cane. Jolted into recognition of physical demise, she
began to cherish the spiritual bonds between her and her

children and grandchildren. Two nights before she died in my grandfather's blue compact car, a block from the hospital, she made dinner for some of the family. She would often spend entire days in the kitchen making gefilte fish and brisket with her one good hand. Those preparations liberated her temporarily from the oppressive sense of completed life. Those dinners in her hot crowded apartment were the closest she came to freedom.

Have I said enough about a world I know better through anecdotes, an occasional narrative, and these movies than through personal experience? I suppose the fictions I invent about their lives, the meanings I invest in their struggles, are no less valid than the antiquated facts of the real history. But watching this film, I sense a truth in their lives that I am afraid to violate; I am afraid almost to offend the fact that they lived.

My father's parents were actually on the dance floor, doing the rumba or waltz! It is a feat I never saw them perform in person. So what if all these people no longer have the inclination to dance. They have all forgotten how to move their feet. These beautiful figures wading and drifting across the screen are not fallen; just older, even dead, victims of the slow and unfanciful depletion of life.

Watching the flickering and euphoric movement of the wedding, I can't help but notice the stupid gaiety of it all. I do not begrudge them their mindless joy, the wedding, the parties, the celebrations in 1945 when they thought that war was over: I don't expect anyone to begrudge me mine. I am not really angry at being shown images of their stupor. So what if they smoked Chesterfields, kissed the bride, wore wide ties with impossible designs on them. So what if they proceeded with the act of living even though they were being cheated out of what was theirs at every moment; out of sons who were to die in the war, but who would rather have stayed home to become acquainted with the pliant and flexuous act of love; out of relatives who died in ovens stoked by men who proved that history did not end last week, but goes on every day. So what if from the distance of thirty years, they seem so profoundly ignorant of their own death and the imminent death around them. It is nine months before Pearl Harbor. In four years, six million of their kind will be gone. But there will always be weddings, and surely the end will catch us all with gin and tonics in our hands.

The lights go on. The lesson is an ambiguous one. Certainly the lesson is not that we shouldn't have weddings or dance or take grandchildren to the zoo on Sunday. I realize that these things are what we salvage from everything else that dies; we preserve the simple continuity of life. No formal tradition, but the casual interplay of generations. To all the people I recognize at the wedding, I am grateful for this: that they chose, and continue to choose, despite tragedies and insanities, despite the fact that they may have forsaken each other, to preserve the wide family. That it mattered to them that we had origins, that it was important to make connections.

Perhaps the lesson is merely that we all die, that it is enough to have lived in the face of death and then simply to have died. Most probably, though, the lesson is this: that it is no longer sufficient just to be together. That, although the movie gives me a sense of continuity, even invincibility, wars *did* occur despite us, massacres were perpetrated despite our anger and the perogatives of life. The lesson is that it is no longer enough to say "We are together" or to say "I do"; that the confirmation of life embodied in my parents' wedding was helpless to stop the affirmation of death everywhere else.

2. In Cambridge, Massachusetts, on a warm April night, large crowds of people occupied Harvard Square, chanting, yelling, sitting on the pavement. Rocks hurtled through the windows of banks and department stores. Riot-squad cops, marching dramatically up a vacated Mass Ave, finally cleared the square with tear gas and clubs, but that inaugurated three or four hours of timorous street fighting. In one of the many

skirmishes taking place in and around the square, the scenario was this: First the cops would charge groups of people in the street, forcing them to flee a few blocks. The kids, soon reassembled at their former position, would then begin to run at the cops, throwing stones, fragments of bricks, taunting them. When they were within twenty yards or so of them, they would stop and run back in anticipation of a police rush. The cops would obligingly disperse them again, perhaps clubbing a few, shooting a tear gas canister or two into a crowd; someone would pick up the canister and heave it back toward the lines of cops. Here I am, standing dangerously close to some Tac squad guys, and they turn on me and my friends suddenly, chasing us into the dorm we live in. We outrun them, fleeing up the stairs to our rooms. The cops, faltering halfway up the stairs because they don't think they should be on Harvard property, leave. Peering around corners, we see that they are gone. We come out, taking to the streets once again where groups of kids are making rushes at the cops who, in turn, force them to retreat.

For hours, they are running back and forth in front of the dry cleaner's and Saks Fifth Avenue, whispering solemn words of encouragement to Radcliffe freshmen who have been gassed. It is different than it was two years before when mothers recoiled in front of their TVs at seeing these girls getting it. Since then, doubts, complicating issues, and words like *repression*, *Weatherman*, and *Vietnamization* have come between them and the central issues. The mothers have long forgotten why their daughters are being gassed and goosed by the cops; all they know is that it is really dangerous now and they want them safe in their arms again. It doesn't appear to matter now if they are gassed or not; its shock value is deflated. The political lesson is lost—the image has been repeated too often to be instructive. The scene is nothing but an elaborate vaudeville act, a laughable facsimile of real hostilities in which each side is content to force the other to one side of the stage and then be chased themselves into the wings. Our feeble attempts to command the streets are nothing but a hoax, a sort of sublimation of the real acts we would like to commit, just as the cops' maneuvers are a sublimation of the authentic repressive tactics they themselves would almost be afraid to use. As it is, not much more really seems at stake than did when I huddled among the trees in my backyard with a cap gun ten years ago, perspiring, waiting for the moment when I could reveal myself to the enemy, get shot in the heart, and demonstrate to him the proper and realistic way to die.

On the streets of Cambridge that night, no one wins and no one loses. There was a time when just our presence on the streets was important. We hoped that this proof of our concern and sincerity would make a difference. We hoped, not so much that we would actually intimidate anyone, but that we would be taken seriously; that our convictions, phrased in the way they were, would speak for those who felt the same way. But instead of calling the government's actions into question, our protest served only to make the monolith more adamant, in the way some criminals only deny their crimes more vehemently when confronted with damning evidence of their guilt. We began to understand we were dealing with men who were not in any way responsive to the needs and painful domestic problems of their country. Not only were our moral arguments spurned by statistics, figments of the technological imagination, but our *moral* arguments were met with *facts* (among them blatant lies) as if morality were based on fact, hence could be challenged by them. Anything to preserve the war. Well, some of us thought, anything to stop the war. And many of these courageous people are now in jail, dead in Chicago, San Francisco, Alabama, around the corner. We were not dealing with a democratic process; we were dealing with utter assholes, men whose moral bankruptcy would soon bring us to tears when their henchmen turned guns on blacks and whites, and fired. So now it is not enough just to be in the streets, to rush the cops and fall back, to send one to the hospital with a broken nose. It is not enough to break a bank window. It is not enough to be content to be together, to be warmed by our mutual bitterness or to hope that the power of our intelligence will in itself be able to overcome their crimes.

Most of that evening, tear gas eddies around me, but I sit on the hood of a car, enraged. I talk earnestly to friends who are coughing badly, asking others who turn up where they've been and what's happening beyond the square. I do not wish I was in the streets burning a police car. That is too easy. Besides, it is an act which does not hit the correct target. I only wish that, having cultivated a sense of justice, I had also cultivated a meaningful sense of action with which to implement it.

In a dream I have of Nixon, I am standing in a sparse crowd of people as he walks by, extending his unctuous hand to well-wishers. As he moves closer to where I am, I approach a level of indignation that is difficult to contain. His head looks like an Idaho potato. I think of all the things I could and want to do. Yet, when Nixon is in front of me, holding out his hand, I shake it, although the taste of vomit is in my mouth.

I come from a class of cowards. The values our lives are structured around are essentially selfish: We promote ourselves, not others, straining to transcend limitations that may not even exist. We lose our ability to act on behalf of others, even to enact what we can only verbalize about our own existence. We don't confront our deficiencies—we merely rise above them. And our impotence loses importance as we move up in a world in which benevolent powerlessness is often a virtue. After our ascent is completed, we look down and realize we are too far away from what should matter to us to do anything about it. We usher ourselves into a bourgeois elite class without assuming responsibility, except in the most abstract, philosophical way, for the welfare of anyone else. We shake our heads at the hopelessness of human affairs, and even though we may ultimately reach down and join a conscientious commission or civil rights association, even though we may take it on the chin from a billy club in the street, we are rarely capable of selfless action.

Cowardice derives from a condition of physical and psychic comfort which makes it irrelevant to take risks. The "Please-And-Thank-You" character of life in my suburb not only rendered life safe, easy, and deceptively self-sufficient, but it gave me the impression that similar justice was being carried out everywhere else in the world. Once I took out a girl from another high school. When I returned her home at three in the morning, her boyfriend, the swarthy star halfback for her high school team, ambushed me in the driveway. I saw him stalking me, coming around to my side of the car. I could hardly misinterpret his intentions, yet I froze. No, I said to myself as he approached me, drawing his hand up into a fist, this thing can be handled peacefully; he's not *really* going to flatten me. Where I come from, we don't throw hands. Listen . . . I'd like to discuss this matter with you. Naturally I was on the ground before I lifted a hand. Bruised, I thanked him for the invaluable lesson he administered: that force is no solution to a problem, but neither is useless negotiation.

The process of submission is inseparable from the process of growing up in the suburbs. Emasculated by our own gentility, we were unable to help ourselves. Allow me momentarily to return to one of the scenes of my baptism, junior high school. The junior high I visited recently was not the one I once attended, but what reason was there to suspect that it was any different than my own, a thousand miles away? It was here that I was weaned and scrubbed in their vinyl bassinets, and I haven't been able to dirty myself since. Here were the narrow tan lockers, the light green and brown tile floors, the closely shaved mathematics teachers, the Art Deco furniture; all preserved through the years, an unwitting museum of nostalgia. The dwarfed nation of students, the knee-high urinals, all attested to the passage of time. The bands of eighth-grade hoydens with their manila complexions and

Pink Pearl eraser thighs attested to my eternal puerility. Most of the boys, still on the verge of their powerful pubescence, flitted down the corridors like frightened birds. Everywhere there were mod clothes and transparent blouses through which enlightened boys could see the over-the-shoulder-boulder-holders. But for the most part, the girls' mothers had endowed them with a seductiveness at an age when they could not yet know what the word means, and it was wasted, except for me and the mathematics teachers who loitered by the drinking fountain between classes, scouting for fresh talent.

After talking to a few morning classes about poetry, I lunched with the faculty in their dining room; the meatless aroma of Bar B Q beef on buns called me back seven years. I selected a sheet of à la carte matzo (a nickel) to go along with my meal and retired to the once forbidden region of the faculty dining room.

During the last four modules of the day, I was sent to the school auditorium to read and talk poetry to a group of a hundred students. PA systems clicked on and off, and suddenly the entire class was on its feet, facing the flag. After the brief ceremony, I perched on a stool in front of them with my notebook of poems; they responded by taking out pencil and paper.

"Put away your paper and pencils," I said in mock anger. "You can't learn anything when you're taking notes." Lord, I sounded just like my seventh-grade English teacher. They turned tentatively to their teachers to see if that was O.K. Then I read them poems which were meant only as short demonstrations of their potential. They, however, in the manner of their education, mistook the poems as inviolable lessons in Literature and Eloquence, things about which they could not care less. I read two poems that concerned a white suburb, similar to their own, hoping that the proximity of the verses to their own lives would open up the poems for them. But they resided too close to their own growth to scrutinize it. If I had only been able to transform my poems into hot meals and nude men and women before their eyes, I would have gladly done so. As I sat before the hundred hairless faces in the aqua and ochre aud, I wanted to try to undo in the hour and a half I had the things that had been done to them in their short lives on Long Island. It would have been wonderful to soil them a bit. But my messianic pretensions soon gave way to the simpler chore of looking at poems with them. But, still, they were so withheld from experience that the poems were to them less a reflection of life than academic exercises they had trained themselves not to understand.

"What do you do," a boy asked, "when you don't write poetry?"

I paused. "I play football, talk on the telephone, kiss girls," I said. A light snicker followed which suddenly made me feel like an aging comedian before an audience of Rotarians. "Poetry, you know, isn't a forty-hour week."

"I have a question," a girl asked from the back. "You always write about things you don't like. But why don't you do anything about them?"

"I don't know why," I replied, "I really don't."

When we were in eighth grade, we slept along with the somnolent decade. Despite an increasingly intrusive media system and the awakening of their older brothers, the enormity of the world is still hidden from these students. Like ourselves, these junior high schoolers continue to suffer from American education's mystification of the world. The world was kept out of our reach no less than aspirin and the facts of sexual intercourse. An educational version of it was, in fact, invented for our benefit. The world was made disproportionately small by our teachers and our textbooks, its inequities ignored, its differing cultures approximated, its messages equivocated, its complexity reduced to a sacrosanct canon of saccharine passages and pictures. It was a world from which textbook writers and educators had effectively exorcised all inferiority and superiority, all ethical dimension. In our history books, other cultures were dealt with almost secondarily. On the other hand, America, like its TV heroes Ward Cleaver and Garfield Goose, survived all calamities and obstacles, fashioning mediocrity into national grace by way of an obtuse patriotism. Other cultures were compared to America's, but with no sense of cultural relativity. Who suspected that the history-book Kodachromes of contented, milk-drinking families and shots of smiling Poles and Latin Americans, and poetry particularly, concealed a quite different truth? We could not furnish counter examples. For all our multiple-choice exams, we never had a real selection.

Perhaps these students are a little better off, more enlightened, more inquisitive. Maybe they are beginning to find it hard to reconcile the world of their education with the one outside. For a few, the awareness is already unwieldy; the problems go beyond puberty, bad grades, small injustices. The vicious secrets of America have been kept almost entirely from them. Their world is both circumscribed and defended by the familiar: their parents, their teachers, their neighborhoods, the Pizza Hut. If they walk all the way home from school on a fair day, they have traversed their universe. They have no idea what an unusual future they are about to come upon. Some already hear a war on the other side of the globe. Next year, they might discover that a few blocks from home there are places they never dreamed of.

Like junior high school, high school taught us to prize obedience and self-aggrandizement. We understood these things to lead swiftly to excellence and success in the world. We questioned neither these ends nor the means. We were all too happy to be singled out for recognition in school, regardless of the distinction. The indignities I suffered in the name of achievement! Once I held the flag at an assembly, standing tall in my madras sports coat before a sea of pale, reverent faces. Once I and a friend were asked to represent the high school at a Kiwanis club luncheon. Both of us sat through the meal stifling laughter at their special songs and handshakes, but the point is that we went. Then there were honors and awards; some of those who won them have not yet recovered. Cheerleading, athletics, student councils, all seem now like diversionary tactics the administration employed to keep us from discovering ourselves. A sentence belonging to John Stuart Mill comes back to me: "The general tendency of things throughout the world is to render mediocrity the ascendent power among mankind." Mediocrity, the denial of extremism in any form, was more than a trend. It was *power.* When I showed up one day senior year attired in modestly bright green corduroy pants, a woman administrator, who never wore a dress manufactured after 1948 and with whom I had charmed myself into a false relationship, stopped and smiled, "When, may I ask, are you going to get out of those ridiculous clothes?" "Mankind," replied Mill, "speedily becomes unable to conceive of diversity when they have been for some time unaccustomed to it."

In high school, we acquired a taste for recognition without having to understand the repercussions of that appetite. There was no failure; if one was unable or unwilling to distinguish himself from others, he just remained part of the mass of well-behaved competents. Ambition was left to those for whom ambition could lead to something else, to the captaincy of a team, to college. Those who came from the less elegant parts of town and who were expected to work at their family's service station or Italian restaurant had no reason to indulge in dreams. While we composed futures for ourselves, their modest fantasies had already been supplanted by realities, survival plans, long evenings in Santori's bar playing pool, and fights at midnight in front of the bank. Instead of recognition in high school, they sought the obscurity that would permit them to pursue their own, less acceptable, activities. There were only those who wanted to get ahead and those who didn't. If you tried to get ahead and failed, life didn't collapse. You were never further away from success than the honor roll, and never further away from failure than Santori's.

Some quit the game altogether, but we decided to come back next week for the grand prize—we went off to college. Harvard. But the preoccupation with recognition was all of a sudden counterpointed by intimations of real failure. For instance, take Cambridge. Cambridge, particularly Harvard Square, was both intriguing and intimidating. There was the possibility of commanding it and knowing it; in high school, we had known our hometowns and the city fathers intimately and commanded them. They loved us for our devotion to their way of life, and we loved them for their devotion to our devotion. The mutual love that grew up was entirely self-serving: It was an excuse for them to throw banquets at us and for us to continually demonstrate our tired affection through small acts of narcissism. If we could just ensure for ourselves the same fame in Cambridge, our lives would be sewn up; we would prove ourselves to be what we always thought we were. We would spend our lives winning attentions, making others happy with selections from our repertoire of good will. We would travel to various cities and remain there until we had made our impression before moving on. We could always enter circles of friends, tell jokes, stay until they laughed obediently and called us by nicknames, and then leave. But Harvard Square promised no such intimacy. We did not know the names of the streets or where to go to buy mucilage. We were stunned by the number of people, of books. We began to believe that history passed through the square, avoiding the rest of America. If we failed to make a dent now, we would never get a chance as we were shuttled into vast and unspecified futures. We now entertained the prospect not of being away from home, but of being lost. Once we had been in danger only of tripping over our small inadequacies. Now, it seemed, we had to stay on our feet or not survive at all.

Not only lost, but stupid. Elsewhere, inferiority could

disguise itself as eccentricity or even as quiet superiority, but not here where eccentricity was a complicated game in itself and superiority meticulously judged. Ah, the threat of being less! So the fight was on, the insistent battle between rising tides of fame and failure. Students who tended toward the extreme took this skirmish too seriously and refused to say hello on the street, trying to convey either excessive arrogance or else humility. It was an absorbing conflict that had so much to do with appearances, poses, and predatory skills that, once again, we forgot what else we could have been doing with our time.

Great men haunted every block of Cambridge; their names were etched into dormitory desks. Precedents became burdensome. Even Chris's Superette had the odor of destiny. After reading so many poems about Cambridge, even good poems, we could never think of Brattle Street in the way we wanted to. Harvard Square was shrouded in so much literature, remembrance, and history that it was less a location than an erected set, a facsimile of the town designed for the production *Histories of Great Men.*

On the tenth floor of Holyoke Center, in Robert Lowell's poetry-writing seminar, fifteen of us sat around a long wooden table, coats draped over the backs of our chairs. We looked outside at the panorama of Cambridge: Mass Ave, Mem Hall, Lehman Hall, University Hall, the distant roofs of Radcliffe, Young and Yee Cantonese Restaurant. It was unfair to us and to the rest of the world that so much vitality (later we might have called it death) should be gathered in one intersection. We leafed through papers, looked at Lowell, a whole class yearning for excellence. We didn't see in the resignation and gentleness of his expression a condemnation of our anxiety and ambition. Some of us edited and wrote the *Advocate,* the literary magazine. Lowell was turned down by the *Advocate* when he was at Harvard. Yet we couldn't imagine becoming great writers unless every honor and privilege was granted us on the way.

A poem was discussed, one written by a student. Soft words concealing sharp criticism came from Lowell; the student's bid for immortality failed. Students offered allusions when they could, trying to outdo each other. Lowell spoke quietly, spreading his hands outward in a sweeping motion, palms down. We all waited for the moment when our poem was to be talked about, waited to be designated, pointed out. Designated as what? As poet-of-the-future, poet-of-the-present, most-likely-to-succeed, anything would do. But we were treated with adultish equanimity by Lowell, by everyone. Although we felt we were on the edge of quality, on the edge of the good poem, we learned that uncertainty was built into everything, that every bit of recognition was accompanied by profound disappointment, even self-disgust, that the whole university experience was a paradox we were called upon to assimilate into the rapidly deteriorating sense of our lives.

Some, with a temperament for competition, acted no less notably now than they had in high school: or much more so. For others who found themselves in the center of this golden stage, the glare was too much; they became frightened, nervously amused, and decided not to perform at all. Slowly, they disclosed their malaise, their inability to cope. There was a shame at not being able to do something better with four years of relative freedom. There was a wish to participate in the world. A pattern of reversal was taking shape. Eager beavers now longed for nothing more than to be constantly intoxicated in billiard parlors. And flaming A-holes quoted Hegel at the proper moments.

We would have liked, some of us, to escape the richness of Harvard, the concentration of things, the density of thought, the involuted lives observing themselves; how nice to be able to reduce our lives to a woman, a meal, a book, a word, a syllable whose sound pleased us. These things would restore the finite, close out the interminable mind. But, as we were about to leave, we would suddenly discover a potential use for our knowledge, or a bit of academic flattery would remind us of what there was to gain by sticking around. Sadly, we saw we were not about to leave college at all.

Beyond doubt, we could locate in the Harvard experience sensations that seemed human: joy, eminence, pride, failure, embarrassment, the Void. But we learned to suspect these feelings because their context was so peculiar and precious. Emotions in Cambridge were too tenuous, not to be trusted. We didn't even feel responsible for them. Like many of our activities, our states of mind were chosen for us.

Harvard and Life rarely seemed to intersect at any point. Sure, indications of Life could be found occasionally: a derelict walking down Plympton Street on Saturday night would startle weekend guests from Wellesley by suddenly whipping it out and pissing without breaking stride; the first snow; the interior of a bus. But what seeped into Harvard Square from the outside world was illumined, like everything else, by that strange light and shimmered, vibrating with self-consciousness.

Were we lucky to be at Harvard, despite our complaints? You bet. But, in the end, it was exactly that element of chance, of determinism, that we now wished to do away with. Instead, we desired to do something on our own, flex some remarkable muscle. But we didn't leave. We stayed on (there would be time later for Life, wouldn't there?). We stayed on, struggling with the (at times equally appealing) possibilities of ignominy and glossy recognition.

Harvard was an auditorium. In it, it was possible to do one of three things. We could perform well, we could perform badly, or we could merely sit in the audience. However, every option, as it turned out, was either too exacting or insufferably boring.

3. Inured to applause, we were not even capable of an unpremeditated, existential act committed for its own sake, committed out of impatience with our inaction. If it wasn't our education, it was our selfishness that prevented us from

letting go. We were so selfish that even freeing ourselves was too generous an act. We talked of all the things we could do and wanted to do, but planning became an end in itself. In reality, we knew nothing, and did less. The affluence of choice gave way to general paralysis.

The most remarkable way in which our poverty of experience was manifested was our tendency to create and fabricate experience. In my hometown, we were never close to active experience, that form of confrontation with the world that implies an intelligent concern with the state of things. No one went off to fight in national wars of liberation, of course. But no one even went off to fight in local wars of liberation. Not enough dropped out of high school when they should have. Actively confronting the absurdity of the high school cosmos would have been a good way to lose votes in the student council elections. Removed from both real poverty and extravagant wealth, we floated idly down the streets of our decorous business districts, anesthetized by the moderation of our lives. We spent little time in ghettos in Chicago, reserving our trips downtown for shopping and weekend dates. During the summer we were tucked neatly into camps or programs or summer schools where the pattern would not be broken.

We began to respond to the vapidity of suburban bourgeois life by seeking, both consciously and unconsciously, experiences we could not genuinely have. Even at the age of twelve or fourteen, I looked upon poverty as somehow honorable, better, a sort of clarification of life. Certain novels I read furnished me with scenes of an impoverished authenticity that I envied. The description of a hungry man gnawing a roll conveyed a sense of survival I was not familiar with, but wanted to approximate. Steinbeck and Hemingway supplied me with images of men in diners and bars. That was all I needed. When I ate dinner alone at home, I would turn off the lights and shovel corn niblets into my mouth, pretending that I was a migrant worker in Salinas. Later, it became important to go constantly to cheap restaurants, by myself or with friends, to eat inexpensively and simulate the experience of indigence.

But it wasn't merely poverty we were after; in addition, there were other sources of life we wanted to know about. For six weeks one summer, I sweated among the cardboard boxes in a warehouse on the South Side. I woke up at six in the morning, dressed, drained a glass of fruit juice and drove an hour to South Ashland Avenue. It was tranquilizing just to be up and driving at that hour down deserted streets, past dark, empty Jewel Food stores. In those soundless dawns, I was conscious of the trees and their bulky movement in the wind. On the highway, the few cars contained workers in khaki shirts, even wearing their hard hats as they drove. By the time I got down to the abandoned stockyards on the South Side, life had begun, motors were growling, the distinct odors of manure and exhaust were rolling in. At the moment I entered the warehouse, a strangeness passed over me, the assumption of a different, humble character; I was in another world. Leon, my fellow worker—that is, the one full-time employee there besides Bob the boss—was already working, his conk piled high on his head, reddened with dye at the tip. He was filling out the first orders, scaling up to the top of cardboard mountains or navigating an orange lift down the dank aisles. Together, we filled orders, loaded boxcars, and sang along to the Delphonics on his combination radio–phonograph. We talked quietly at lunch, which we often ate together at a nearby playground, discussing the areas of knowledge intersected by both our lives; occasionally, we threw a football around, feeling some strange spiritual proximity when we played catch. I figured Leon was around my age, eighteen or nineteen. I usually brought a couple of tuna fish salad sandwiches or chopped liver on rye or salami and cheese down to work. Leon only ate peanut butter on Wonderbread every day, constantly refusing my offers to share my lunch. When I discovered that Leon was twenty-seven and had two kids, our relationship altered. When we played touch football after that, I always went out for the passes.

> The idea of an outer world that should match our inner
> world is the visual book man's ideal.
>   —Marshall McLuhan, *Culture Is Our Business*

We didn't always go to bars to drink; we went to bars to be
there at the counter, eating fried bacon rinds. We looked for
situations where the assembly of people was most arbitrary
and the change of scene most frequent; it was the way to escape the memory of suburbs whose props were immobile and
changeless. It is no wonder we became fond of El trains and
subways which joined a random selection of humanity with
fast motion. We felt closest to these sources when we were
speeding between stops with the other dour and fixed faces.
We agitated our lives when we could, calling friends up long
distance from booths somewhere in Iowa, hitchhiking, finally
running down to the river, our eyes alive with dope. We
apotheosized normal occurrences. Too well-read, we had long
ago forfeited any chance to fully participate in sensual experience—we only strove to emulate fictional characters. Literature helped us to select good experiences and then to know
how to describe them so that they could be resurrected in an
instant. But, at the same time, literature taught us to be conscious of our experiences, to know they were taking place. We
began to narrate our own lives, saying to ourselves as we
walked into a bar in Boston, "Now he walks into the bar, out
of the quiet rain, where he is suddenly among neon signs over
the counter and the moist chatter of the patrons. Slowly taking off his raincoat, shaking the water off it, he sits down and
orders a dark beer." We may even have gone so far as to track
down experiences to have primarily for the sake of being able
to remember them. We would begin to reminisce about an
event or sensation that was still taking place. This kind of
instant nostalgia made it hard to immerse ourselves in anything we were doing.

We became so adept at substituting fabricated experiences
for real ones that we forgot real ones had to be earned; we
wanted immediate experience. In movies, the emotional

homecoming scene of a soldier returning from the war will transmit a strong feeling of pride, renewal, etc. We, watching the film, recognize only that moment of arrival and not the two years the soldier spent overseas which give that moment its full meaning. Movies can be evocative even though they truncate experience; one doesn't have to show, or even allude extensively, to the soldier's two years abroad in order to develop sentiment. We longed for the incisive moment, the coming home, wanted it without the two years that went before. We wanted to be treated as workers without being workers. We wore work pants, even though our wallets bulged in the back pockets. We wanted our poetry published when we weren't even proud of the poems. We thought all one had to do to be part of a cause was to be sympathetic to it. We wanted to linger at the precarious peak; we refused to fall over the edge and hear ourselves clatter as we hit the ordinary. We wanted applause without having performed. We demanded notoriety from suburbs which had groomed us to be weaklings.

We denied our affluence vigorously, trying to exist outside our city limits; but, in fact, we rarely got close to those alternative experiences we induced. By satisfying us with resemblances, our flirtations made it even more difficult than ever to appreciate or understand poverty, for instance. Our downward mobility was a game. The experiences for us were invariably enjoyable, even at their most destitute; after all, it was nice to "broaden our horizons."

But we weren't so innocent that we thought the workers were enjoying the romantic experience of being workers. (We weren't so selfish that we thought that only we, the middle class, was being robbed.) For those who peopled our experiences, the workers we sat next to at the quaint bars we frequented, we understood fully that it was, alas, a different story. We wished not so much to be them as to drain for ourselves the modest glories of their situation.

The hope of becoming anything but what we were, well-read members of the bourgeois class, grew increasingly dim. But perhaps it would have been possible to penetrate an alien experience had we chosen to stay there awhile. We had friends who went off to Guatemala and weren't heard from or who went off to make bombs and died in their own explosions. Instead, though, our decision was to alight momentarily on foreign objects and then return to our proper homes.

Soon everything, including the inescapable experience of being middle class, seemed false. Was the question then of a real or natural experience a mirage? Did those who found themselves in Guatemala feel that their experience was more or less consonant with their destinies than what they had known before? Did one have to travel longer and longer distances in order to feel at home? Certain experiences were more difficult for us, but did they seem less or more real because we had to struggle to master them? We were ultimately faced with the twin possibilities that either every experience is real, no matter how vicarious or secondhand or, in what amounted to the same proposition, no experience is real.

[Des Esseintee] believed that the imagination could provide a more than adequate substitute for the vulgar reality of actual experience . . . it is well known that nowadays, in restaurants famed for the excellence of their cellars, the gourmets go into raptures over their rare vintages manufactured out of cheap wines treated according to Pasteur's method. Now, whether they are genuine or fakes, these wines have the same aroma, colour, and bouquet and the pleasure experienced in tasting these factitious, sophisticated beverages is identical with that which would be afforded by the pure unadulterated wine, now unobtainable at any price.

There can be no doubt that by transferring this ingenious trickery, this clever simulation onto the intellectual plane, one can enjoy, just as easily as on the material plane, imaginary pleasures similar in all respects to the pleasures of reality . . . no doubt that without stirring out of Paris it is possible to obtain the health-giving impression of sea bathing—for all that

involves is a visit to the Bain Vigier, an establishment to be
found on a pontoon moored in the middle of the Seine.
                                    —J. K. Huysmans, *A Rebours*

Whether social climbing, social descending, or merely trying to be ourselves, we had the sensation of losing our balance.

Now, some of us seem to be inventing the experience of
revolution (if the experience is *real* in any case, it nonetheless
can be *contrived*). We haven't invented the need for some
sort of revolution or some of the conditions for it which may
already exist, but our response to the challenge of societal and
political change has been conditioned by the past, and we are
likely to look upon the matter of revolution as only another
excursion into exciting, foreign territory. Unquestionably,
there are sincere revolutionaries in this country (not necessarily good or effective, but *sincere*) who have shown their
commitment to change through physical acts rather than
rhetorical promise. But while they have been taking care of
business, too many other self-professed revolutionaries have
done nothing to prove their concern but memorize the critical
cant of the New Left and fill the streets at appropriate moments. While some have put their lives in danger, others demanding the same political respect have joined only the cult
of the revolution—adopted dress, stances, everything but the
revolution itself—and sought to conceal their inactivism with
a borrowed, superficial activism.

Those revolutionaries whose energies have been deflected
in more passive, cultural directions by Yippie influence, for
instance, must simply admit to themselves that they are not
part of the avant-garde political revolution. Yet revolution has
become so fashionable that even young men selling radical
clothing have mastered the language of the underground and
claim to be in the forefront. Once upon a time, a couple of
years ago, everyone including the haberdasher was welcomed
into the movement. It was wonderful to know we would all
be at rallies and on marches. The more the better; as our numbers grew, war and idiocy would surely come to an end. That

early feeling of community on college campuses spoke of soli-
darity and social change.

But that community is gone. In its early stages, the vague
cultural–political movement looked like a constructive, am-
bitious force. Hope was based on the promises of each con-
tingent (hippies, Yippies, politicos) to do their part. In the
last two years, though, radical political groups have been mortally wounded by sectarianism, and some countercultural projects have begun to look like any other fad, content to absorb
as many witless college-age people into their stylized indo-
lence as they can. Instead of actively confronting American
culture, many people never really got beyond the verbal level
of dissent. Even aimless, physically violent trashings were just
incoherent translations of semiarticulate arguments. What
people wanted to effect was never accomplished, only crudely
illustrated in the streets. Now that urban communities like
Cambridge are beginning to resemble ghettos, the freedom
desired by so many street people from upper middle class
backgrounds reveals itself to be very easy to achieve. Their
dropping-out has not entailed great risks for themselves, and
they have eschewed a radically productive life, discontinuing
their struggle in favor of a repetitious statement of languor
and defeatism. In theory, they embody the admirable radical
unwillingness to submit themselves to any authority, but, still,
they are content to loll while more sincere radicals are struggling desperately to find programs for their lives, they under-
mine the best efforts of their own friends. Living off an urban
environment which is already unable to support its congeni-
tally poor inhabitants, street people perpetuate an illness they
condemn in the abstract. They live off their brothers as well
as the establishment, panhandling indiscriminately in the
name of no movement or cause beyond their own appetite
and a sort of dissent by sensation. They have enervated those
who take the question of honest, radical survival seriously.
They have parasitically used the diligent aspects of the movement. Riding to mendicancy on the wave of activism, they

have taken everything and contributed nothing but meager and predictable proof that one can live freely off America, at least temporarily.

More and more radical lives appear to be poses. If one can succeed emphatically in a pose, fine; it may even be a *real* experience. But I suspect our ability, in general, to move beyond the first premise, to move beyond the easier acts of negation and confrontation. Intellectually, we may have completed the process and conceived of a final radical destination; we have made propositions for our escape. But when someone opens the door, we are ensconced in our upholstered living rooms, afraid to leave.

Although the charge can truly be leveled only at the soft, sycophantic radicals, John Aldridge has announced the highest irony of all:

> . . . Even their interest in feelings and soul, like their infatuation with Tarot cards and Eastern mysticism, is not so much a sign of religious consciousnes as another form of their search for mechanistic solutions—in this case, a kind of easy-to-assemble, do-it-yourself metaphysics which, once constructed, will "explain" or cure the complicated problems of being. . . . Thus, one can see how the young would be obliged to take only a very slight tuck in their thinking in order to move quite happily into the brave new world now in the process of being created by technocracy, a world in which all problems will be solved by social engineering, all injustices erased by benevolent legislation, and all qualitative values declared irrelevant—very probably by law.
> —John Aldridge, *In the Country of the Young*

The community is gone because people have suffered the idealism of a collective goal. Not having a program wasn't the difficulty (that is a meaningless objection that everyone to the radicals' right has conjured up). It was a question of not enough people having and pursuing projects of personal salvation. Despite the opportunities for individual justification in an irrational world, there was and is a refusal to perfect one's own life. Instead, people are content to preserve the disorder in their own houses while hoping that an SDS meeting or street epiphany will conveniently decide for them a liberating and common future. People have too long deferred to the abstracted, invented experience of revolt, instead of simply making a personal commitment. The promise never to eat hot dogs, to help support a poor family in America, to think about violence and how it should or shouldn't be used, the promise even to admit the impossibility of promising: anything but the vain and generalized illusion of a dehydrated revolution we can water with our gestures. Although one of the tacit purposes of radical confrontation is to create self-consciousness in the opponent, we have forgotten to take a good look at our own posture.

So the movement has broken down into smaller autonomous groups. The community may be gone, but the movement remains as a variety of more insular cabals. Some, expressing themselves quietly and physically, have begun to distinguish themselves from others. Others, understanding that viable counterculture does not mean the lifeless negation of the existing order, look to their own honesty and aesthetic sense for strength. And all are beginning to distinguish themselves from that amorphous, temperamental group of disaffected, dull Americans, from teeny-boppers, fair-weather insurgents, and those who observe the school year and their own fickle inclinations. If circumstances are favorable, in the streets! If not, to the tennis courts, the libraries, abroad to sightsee. We may be as far away from revolution as we are from poverty.

> Direct your rage to those who cause it. Don't try to run away from your pain. Find its causes and smash them.
>   —Paul Nizan

It may be that the only effective antidote to our own cowardice and to the acts of our government is intelligent vio-

lence. Violence is abhorrent. But it is the horrible secret that
government has disclosed and now it belongs to all of us. The
government will begin to pay for its countless murders. Those
measured acts of violence (is *physical aggression* a more accurate term?) that debilitate the efforts of American foreign
policy without expending human life may become the only
valid political acts at our disposal. This violence (the target of
which is the property and proceedings of the government, not
human life) will take place outside the longer, evolutionary
process that will, over the years, account for our revolution.
Rather than a cohesive plan of attack, these are acts of retribu-
tion for the government's crimes, perhaps the only response
left to us after their refusals to admit or apologize. If we are
smart, we already know that any coordinated long-term project of violence will be easily defeated by the government, but
individual acts, statements of disgust and nausea, may save
our lives and dignity. Jesse Jackson, himself nonviolent, may
have suggested the course of intelligent violence in a speech
delivered at Harvard in the spring of 1970: "Are we going to
lie still and quiet in the whale [the system] and let the whale
wail on or are we going to use our madness without method
and drive the whale to deeper water where we will all drown
—or are we going to give our madness a method and grab the
whale by his vital organs and direct him to shallow waters?"
Peaceful assemblies and rallies are not only demonstrably futile now, but they deceive participants into believing they
have a hand in the revolutionary process.

The lingering war and domestic conditions and loitering
stupidity in this country have created a moral elite for whom
violence is no longer an unthinkable strategy. What is unthinkable is continuing to submit passively to our own un-
doing. (If we are not already part of this country's spectacular
demise, we have been doing nothing more than watching the
descent from a folding chair.) A government whose global
prominence is ensured largely through the use of program-
matic violence invites at the very least the element of coercion

on the part of its own dissenting countrymen. Seriously, how
much do they think we can take? How will the argument that
violence itself, in any form, is untenable answer to the massacres, the most blatant violence of all, that our government has
perpetrated and sponsored in Southeast Asia alone, and refused always to punish legally, even acknowledge? And how
many babies and lobotomized veterans will it take before we
can show to this government its own work?

5. I am back home now. Outside my bedroom window, the
sound of crickets heaves noisily. Except for that, the night is
given over to silence and a black opacity. I become aware of
myself in my chair. I am studying certain papers on my desk,
among them orange note cards. On the first shelf above my
desk, my mechanical plastic watermelon man rests in front of
Madame Bovary. In my pen cup, there is an Easterbrook
fountain pen, a black Flair, a yellow retractable Bic I bought
in France in 1966, a turquoise Parker Jotter, a brown Pentel,
a black Mr. Sketch watercolor pen, a retractable Eversharp
ball point with a clear plastic section, a Venus 365 ball point,
and six plastic lead pencils made in Taiwan. There is a message
on the pencil cup which says, Be Sharp. It reminds me of the
time I left a coffee shop in Denver, and the waitress said,
"Come again." On the wall, there are a few watercolors. There
is a letter from my editor and an empty Player's cigarette
packet pinned up. I count a certain number of books on my
shelf and then compute what percentage of them I have read.
Here on a sheet are the batting averages of my freshman baseball team in high school. I batted .244, 76 points below my
average in my senior year.

After a while, I suffocate in these details. I cannot decon-
gest my past, though it is hardly inscrutable. Furthermore, no
one has yet meddled with it. Posters have not been moved
since 1963 or '65. Things are in place. What would it have
been like if they had been moved? Perhaps I would have been
a different person, batting .315 freshman year, .403 senior

year, being farmed out to Fargo after graduation for two years to play class-B ball while my aging father and mother drove 180 miles each weekend to watch me pitch. When I lost the zip on my fast ball, I joined the army. How was I to know what it would be like? At Fort Lewis, Washington, I slept in the barracks next to a guy who has played in the minors, and we would talk softly after lights out about games in which we had played and maybe starred. Often, we would talk about girls; not crudely, but affectionately, about the ones we had left behind. When I told him I had only had one girl, he laughed a little into his pillow, but I never knew whether that meant he had had many more than me or not. We put up posters of the Zombies and Tony Oliva in our lockers and once we went to Tacoma with a couple other guys to drink and get laid. I got drunk, but the face of my whore was sad and it made me unhappy and I left and walked around until the others were done.

Boot camp was hard, and I began to wonder why I was there. Often you would catch guys masturbating in the showers, their backs to the door. They would always do it and also take shit from the sergeant. My friend and I stuck together and had fun when we could, and we didn't get in trouble. He once told me he hoped he would go to Nam soon because he couldn't wait to kill a gook, he was so bored at Fort Lewis. I told him I never wanted to kill anyone, but he said I had no choice now. Five weeks after we got over, my right leg was blown off. You understand? I'm not simply saying "my right leg was blown off." My right leg was blown off. Looking down right now at where it used to be, I assure you it was blown off. That was the one I used to push off the rubber with. When it was gone, I would lie in bed and actually feel it. I would actually feel my leg moving, toeing the rubber, driving off the rubber, and then coming up high behind my left leg and down to the base of the mound. I would wriggle my toes under the sheets. But then I would look under and see that I had no toes. I had no foot or leg. Halfway down my thigh it stopped and there was nothing else. I only looked at the stump once before it was sewn up. I lunched, so to speak. The doctor said to me shortly after they fixed me up that it would be awhile before I could play ball again, and he laughed. He said, Don't take it too hard because there are a lot of guys who would be happy to have lost only a leg. I told him to fuck off. The funny thing about losing a leg is that it really doesn't hurt that much. There's nothing to hurt. It's just not there. I told them in the hospital that I wanted to see my leg, that I wanted it sent home with me. But they said that they had thrown it away. They had tossed it out with all the other legs and arms and faces.

When I got home, everyone made a big deal about seeing me again. To tell you the truth I didn't want to see them very much. But they gave parties for me and asked me to tell them exactly what happened over there, which I refused to do. My parents bought me a Rambler American and wanted to buy me a plastic leg but I said no thanks. My girl was there, and all I wanted to do was to make love to her and forget, but she wouldn't at first with my leg and all, and it was two months before she wanted to sleep with me. By then, something had happened to me and I was acting funny, staying by myself. While we were in bed one night, I realized I didn't have a right leg and I said to her to stop, you don't want to have sex with a guy with only one leg. She started to cry and she wouldn't stop. I finally told her to go home. I must have been screaming by then. She left and that was the last time I saw her.

Or suppose that there were Scripto pens and pencils in my pen cup instead of an Esterbrook and my room faced west instead of east. I batted .275, swinging into the number-three spot. There were once many Socialists in my family, union organizers in the thirties who were beaten by the cops, but later became respectable lawyers. Though my parents wanted me to go to a good university and I had the marks to do so, I pretty much refused to do whatever it was they wanted me

to. As a result, I did a lot of things against my better judgment; destroying draft-board documents was not one of them.
At the moment, I'm hiding in Maryland. I'll take off soon,
but I think the FBI will get me eventually. That doesn't
bother me, except that there are so many better things to do.

But I am the one who batted .244 freshman year and .320
senior year. I am the one who lost his starting job at first base
halfway through the freshman season in college for smoking
a Hav-A-Tampa after a training meal; I am the one who, in
his last two trips to the plate in organized baseball, doubled
and tripled, and raised his average to .237. I am the one who
said good-bye to baseball and to his virginity and who is hiding at the moment in his hometown in his carpeted room
among the minor trophies of his childhood. I am the one who
out of the depths of his well-being, out of the depths of his
health and youth, out of his wealth and early wisdom, cries
out for some air.

Yesterday, I walked through the business district, visiting
the merchants who furnished me for years with the parapher-
nalia of adolescence. Into the stationery store for binders and
folders and inks, into the clothing store for V-necks and the
drugstore for Mr. Goodbar, into the ice-cream parlor, the
hobby shop, and the delicatessen. Into all the stores where I
gleefully equipped myself for episodes of my own disintegra-
tion. I would have liked to close my eyes and leave that moment, that innocuous yet disgusting moment in front of the
Burger Bar. To leave this somewhat final stage of the civilization of the individual; from Warsaw to Chicago to this suburb, the decrescendo finally reaching the exhausted state of
sobriety. Nothing happens here; everything militates against
action, against collision with unforeseen objects. Everyone
quietly escapes even the intimation of disturbance, shying
away from the aggressive saleswoman in the fashion shop. Inside the Burger Bar, a burger is being served. On the wall, the
faintest, clumsiest reminder of history—a lacquered Bosch
print. To return to the scene of my averted future, and still

find nothing. Yet, I am fond of this moment, even though I can't breathe in it, because it is only against the deenergized suburban panorama that I can measure any of my own meek actions and come out on top. To feel myself grating against this recent past is a sign of hope. It is a weak statement of intent and power, I confess, but I thrive, if I thrive at all, on its death. So perhaps I would have liked to leave that instant, awakening in a moment of my own making. Perhaps I had no desire to leave at all. Deciding to remain, I have no cures for it. I have my hands full standing close enough to the patient to observe the spectacle of death, but far enough away to avoid contracting the fatal disease. I am the curator of a condition I detest. Even if I close my eyes, when I open them, I am where I always was, waiting for the lights to change at the corner of Laurel and St. John's.

A car pulls up next to me, and the driver yells over to me. It is a girl with whom I went to high school. She has filled out in the intervening years, her body softening at the edges. In the back seat, I glimpse a row of grocery bags. The light is still red, so I am obliged to return surprise at the meeting and the pleasantries which follow. I am piqued in an instant, true to my inclination to spare most deviants from any other class while condemning any member of my own class who has done exactly what was expected of him. She is married now, living a few blocks from her parents, ready to model her future children's lives after her own. Maybe this is the girl I thought of asking out to the Kick-Off dance sophomore year. Maybe this is the same girl I wanted to ask out or drive home or longed to fondle passionately in the bus foyer sixth period. Perhaps she is the one to whom I once chose to confess intricate secrets, leaning against the wall at the dance after the basketball game, my arm barely brushing her shoulder. Is she the one who wrote on the inside flap of my yearbook a short message which ended "Luv ya!"? I don't recall; I only know that she is now married and no longer wishes to be fingered in the parking lot or to be a social worker or a nurse or to do something which would at least be remembered by close friends. The light turns green. Her desires are finally confined to the sluggish facts of her life and no one else's. I have the impulse to suddenly jump into her car and molest her viciously, kneading her tits until they are blue. But she is already off, turning left, her arm dangling out of the car window.

When we were younger, a friend and I used to play Things We Should Have Done, a game which consisted only of elaborately describing to each other what we had wanted to do in situations that had just passed and found us doing nothing. Marveling at the ingenuity of our schemes at the kitchen table, we almost forgot that we had failed to follow them through.

I think of the wedding film. What is peculiar about the movie is that it ends unexpectedly. It doesn't end with a shot of the bride and groom standing with their parents before a dark satin curtain or with my father's hand holding my mother's which is grasping a knife to cut the wedding cake. No, the photographer is once again at the buffet table, shooting a group of people. A man appears to be talking, telling a story. There is a crumb of cake on the corner of his mouth. He suspects nothing, least of all that film is running out, least of all that a decision is about to be made which is beyond his control. He is in the middle of a sentence and begins to raise his right hand to emphasize a point. A woman adjusts her dress.

Go Away Richard Brautigan, You're
Not Helping College Poetry Any

all-beef: consisting of prime steer beef, as in a good steak.
all-meat: consisting of any unspecified meat, including horse
and cat meat, as in all-meat wieners, bad bologna, and
luncheon loaf.

1. Terms

Beginning early in 1968, Wesleyan Press, which has cod-
dled, fondled, and taken great pains to discover and publish
young American poets, began a biannual college poetry an-
thology entitled *Alkahest*.[1] Since its inception, *Alkahest* has
appeared (three) times, making available on a national scale
a selection of previously unpublished undergraduate verse. It
is not a publication you might easily pick up and read since it
has benefited from neither wide publicity nor acclaim. Yet,
despite the fact that it is an obscure periodical, plagued by
unattractive student art work and a slim audience, *Alkahest*
offers a fair representation of contemporary college poetry,
which is an overpopulated and underscrutinized field.

This last statement is not as empty as it might sound. After
having read countless student poetry manuscripts at two Ivy

[1] The poetry extracts within this chapter are quoted from *Alkahest* (numbers
2 and 3), Wesleyan University Press, 1968, 1969 and are reprinted by permission.

League schools, I feel on intimate terms with our peculiar idiom and some of our tendencies as well as our capacity to produce vast quantities of fatty, all-meat verse. However, I do sense that my taste buds have been dulled rather than sharpened by the consumption of so much student work, making it, in the end, difficult to judge delicately. Frankly, my palate's confused. If you eat a hundred all-meat burgers, and among them, one all-beef patty, you will not notice the all-beef patty.

Victimized by overeating then, and the lack of a detached perspective, the critical obligation becomes one of attempting to characterize rather than make specific judgments of college poetry now. Premature and untutored literary judgments have unquestionably, when written by critics of influence, helped to banish potentially good writers from our body of literature while admitting others most would prefer to have never heard from at all. As always, it seems that the particular dispositions of some editors tend to obscure solid verse while elevating fetishists and high school orators to prominence, a position from which they will embarrass us when they finally appear on the "Tonight Show" and write short pointless reviews of their friends' pointless first books.

Cooking Directions: Place frozen Brussels Sprouts in a saucepan; add ½ cup water and ½ tsp. salt. Bring to a boil, reduce heat and simmer covered, 8–10 minutes, or until Brussels Sprouts are just tender. Drain and serve.

If we can have sprouts in ten, how long do you figure any one of us is going to spend perfecting dactyls? When directed in creative-writing courses to produce a poem, more likely than not we retire to the kitchen where we baste some prefabricated emotion with a new vocabulary and type it out. It is no surprise that we write poems in an hour, which many college students do. We may be incorrigible romantics in some ways, but our emotion is more often recollected frantically than in tranquillity, between classes in a Spiral notebook more often than on long, contemplative walks. Wordsworth, it is said, was often unable to break off composition in his head as he walked in the countryside. I have a friend who walks for hours with his hands in his pockets and is unable to start it.

When our parents, as children, struggled with quatrains, they must have been diligent, if not skillful, about it. Presumably, the bygone era of courting, coy dialogues, and parlors with Victrolas both engendered and perpetuated a more deliberate way of life. Cynicism was not in fashion. Our parents applauded a type of elegance we find ludicrous today. They may not have thought Joyce Kilmer's "Trees" was great, but I doubt that many thought it was bad.

Something has happened to us. Halfway through lectures, we start to squirm in our seats. We suspect we are losing our minds. But our self-indulgence is not a choice we have made so much as a necessity. The substance of lectures loses meaning on the edge of the abyss; what seems to save us from falling is not self-discipline, not submission to the forces that only bring us closer to lobotomy, but rather a reclamation of the individual powers we once gave up in exchange for entrance into the universities of our choice. We have to squirm, to resist, to refuse to read books. It is not simply that we have the leisure which allows us to be discontented with the moderate competency too often mistaken for something better; we now claim the right. Hopefully, in a few decades when we will have become the objects of our own critique and our children, staging demonstrations of peace, will tell us so, we will listen to them and hold on less tenaciously to our own "excellences."

As it is, we are already losing grip on those "excellences," and admitting that poetry is difficult, especially in what resembles a prerevolutionary age. We're impatient with the process of poetry. We've grown impatient with the Richardsian textual analysis we absorbed in high school. Now that many of us have mastered it to a good degree, we believe we don't need it. We are determined, in part, to create poems which defy close examination. In poetry, as in many areas, we have begun to conspire against the snappy logic politicians are using to keep us in wars and administrators are using to keep us in schools.

As we bring our poetry closer to our lives, we understand that our poetry should be no more comprehensible than our lives, which are a mystery to us. If our lives are fast, our poetry must be fast too. But if, in fact, one of the major reasons we spend little time perfecting our poems is that we spend little time perfecting our lives, we're in trouble. The Problem is this: We must spend more time. It's a well-known argument that this age has quickened most facets of our lives and that this maddening acceleration has fueled very facile critiques of society. Saying that good quality is impossible is often the next step, to say that under the conditions we must expect and accept the cursory, the built-in obsolescence, and the carelessly spontaneous. We must be satisfied with instant poetry; after all, Instant Quaker Oats tastes just as good as the regular stuff. But if, in fact, life in a velocitized world is one of the chief reasons we are writing prolific rubbish, it becomes our duty not to capitulate, but to resist and begin to write more careful poetry, drive more slowly, and brush our teeth longer and more often.

2.

I have a friend who makes leather handbags. He goes down to the dark leather district in Boston, by South Station. There, in a basement office, Mr. Segal sells him hides which he takes back to his room, where he designs and hand-sews his bags before taking them to sell on the street. Hawking his bags with him awhile ago, I enticed a college coed. The price was eighteen dollars. That's too much, she said, I know where I can get a bag like that for twelve. I know, I said, but those are machine-sewn and there are a thousand like it in this city alone, all from the same factory. The reason this one costs eighteen dollars is that it's hand-sewn. It took hours, not minutes, to create; and its human imperfections make it unlike any other in the world. Oh, she blinked, confused by my polemic, but eighteen dollars is half again the cost of the others.

It seems there is less and less among young poets and young readers an interest in the poem's genesis, in the hard history that a poem's final and ostensibly effortless execution conceals. Valèry once said that no poem is ever finished, it's only abandoned. We should appreciate and encourage the struggle that goes on by thinking of the poem not as a flawless finale, but rather as a stopping point on the way to perfection. The poem is the point at which our strength gave out. Instead of staying beside the poem for as long as we can, it seems that our ambitions for each poem are so low that we can safely excuse ourselves after a few hours or a couple of drafts.

3. We Envision the End

Too often written in the throes of neurosis or milder malaise, student poetry frequently becomes self-referential confession in which autobiographical fact is too often passed off as metaphor or, at its lyrical peaks, is a description of minor apocalypse. Influenced by the Confessionalist tendency to identify with the illnesses of the entire era, we are prone to throw up our hands at the slightest ontological difficulty:

> They assemble, the sleepwalkers
> at the edge of the world . . .
> And the fall defies calendars,
> an infinite floating.

The apocalypse can be a simple thing, too sadly final to admit analysis or even description, as in an *Alkahest* poem titled "Goodnight to Dylan Thomas":

> The light began to dim.
> You did not rage.
> Sensible only at the end,

you left the Chelsea Hotel,
walked across the street;
died.

Never straying far from contemporary concerns, the end is
even seen in faintly ecological terms:

he has nowhere
to go

huge dark owls
pass gracefully over his head
but the other animals,
soft and white,
have not been seen there
in years.

or suggestively:

death, I think,
is like a thimble, she said
smiling
she wore a red dress
and we danced another waltz
she didn't know
that death is like a window

Yet, beneath all our private horrors, there is an echoing
humor, almost flippancy. Unable to really understand war, we
cannot always take our fear seriously. The draft lottery implies an untouchable fate so remote from Western logic that
many of us don't realize what's at stake. Turning uneasily to
our friends, we laugh. We are not Wilfred Owens; we are able
to handle our end from a comfortable distance:

Luckily, then, I hear that a few miles
from death there's a Cantonese restaurant
where we can have some barbecued pork
and talk.

Having never been close to the palpable apocalypse of the Second World War, we seem anxious to invite into our poems the
disasters our good fortune has deprived us of. Our joking,

when we write lightly of the end, is not the uneasy joking of war veterans trying to forget their losses; it is the uneasy joking of those who, born during an advanced stage of national atrophy, see the subtler dissipations of American life and figure something more climactic can't be far behind. Conveniently, though, our black humor, by displaying tragic moments in the light of their amusing inevitability, only apologizes for our passivity. We tend toward the wry formulation, the monotonous statement of the end, rather than the agonized appraisal, the serious attempt to avert it. Our poems don't prepare for the future; they merely describe it.

4. We Write Short Poems

If we deliberately eschew the technical concerns of poetry (although we are often well-versed in them), ' get the impression that many spend the gained time achieving a lyrical reticence. Of the ninety poems in the second and third issues of *Alkahest*, no less than half are under twelve lines long. Inevitably, this practice leads to epigrammatic rather than discursive poetry. Many college poets not only admire and enjoy Richard Brautigan, but identify with him and his shotgun lyrics. The success he has had doing what he does is irresistible (although the influence of the short poem hardly begins with Brautigan). He infests his poems with a highly personal idiom that approximates rather than communicates feeling. He approaches that extreme of style and ambiguity which justifies almost any reaction to his poems. Note: Implicit in his poetry is the form that makes our politics good but our poetry often negligent. A short poem in *Alkahest* which ends, "Good bye little old lady,/ There will be no loud parties/ In the rest home." derives its interest and meaning only from the irony of those last three lines and not from the poem as an organic whole. As the punch line is delivered, we discover that the preceding stanzas are there merely for the sake of the conclusion.

When I'm talking to someone
I'm really as quiet as a sleeping house;
I creak and the people sleeping in me
Wake and listen
And wait for the noise to stop.

The gifts have not arrived
and my ear hurts.
Lets forget ugly things.

Listen, Joey, you're ninety-seven years old.
In three years you're going to be a hundred.
Why do you feel like dancing,
    like you're a kid of sixteen,
    with it all ahead of you?

The three passages above are all complete poems. We know
how to make slight, even gratuitous, poems attractive. We
know a trick or two.

5. We Use Slang

"The end is at hand,"
I scream . . . reaching up, I grab her
where it counts and begin to believe it.

Perhaps we owe to all the rock n' roll lyrics we've memorized the temptation to invoke witty, idiomatic, musical
speech patterns. Whatever the source, one of the most salient
characteristics of student poetry is conversationality, our
familiarity, at times almost irreverent, with the language. Increasingly, our poems are not lyrical asides, preceded by a
pause and delivered in a more-sonorous-than-usual voice. Our
poems have become part of our general idiom, often indistinguishable from our sense of humor. If we are not exactly
careful with the language, we insist on feeling close to it. In
a short *Alkahest* poem which exemplifies the Brautiganese
popular among students, the poet, like the comedian, makes
elaborate preparations for his punch line:

> my daughter is gaining
> more motor control—
> today she pinned my
> penis pronglike, with
> thumb and forefinger,
> like a frog down on
> a dissecting table—
> and relit that ancient
> fire in my wife's eyes.

Now this is good, more eloquent an example than the last, but still we can't wait to get to the end to get to the joke. Nothing arrests us halfway through, startling us with its autonomous beauty.

6. We Use Falling Cadences

Some have perfected the dying fall, the subtle drop in the last stanza, the ironic understatement, the receding rhythm like a rock bounding down a mountainside, da-Da da-Da da-Da da-Da da-Duh. Unfortunately, as a result, much of our poetry has become predictable in that we know that the rock hitting bottom always signals the end of the poem. Few really have the time or energy to push, like Sisyphus, their poems uphill.

Our music is dying, dissonant, at its very best haunting, and that is fine. But in the process, many have forgotten how to say anything without being ironic, and that is bad. We don't have to turn toward Edna St. Vincent Millay, but we should turn away now and then from our own verbal cuteness.

7. We Prefer Studebakers to Cars

In general, we write with a high substantive level; that is, with a good degree of specificity, of name-calling, with an eye and ear for the juxtapositions of countraries, for poetic *tension*. An expression of our substantive concern is our search for interesting objects, the selection of the exact physical fact. In the ninety poems in the last two *Alkahests,* oboes appear twice. More common objects like corn flakes and orange soda show their faces, but *Alkahest* contributors also come up with "Va. Sweet Grille," "Cloemana City," "Rice Chex," "saguaro cactus," and "Engine 10–9–0." The sun is no longer pasted in the sky like a red wafer. It rises like a "ping-pong ball."

8. We Universalize Experience

An interesting technique which appears in much poetry, and which derives perhaps from Eliot's work, is the collective image. The poet, by presenting a singular or individualized detail in the form of a plural image, can make it appear to be a universal experience. In this way, Eliot's "lonely men in shirt-sleeves, leaning out of windows" becomes an image we almost appropriate as our own. If Eliot had spoken of "the lonely man in shirt-sleeves, leaning out of the window," we would have deferred to the poet, thinking he had a particular man in mind whom we could glimpse only through the poem. But, by making the image plural, he has given us the opportunity to see its elements in our lives. Of course! We too have seen those men leaning out of the windows and that scene, recovered from our experience, is what we think of. Our experience becomes identical to that of the poem. The poet, in making the experience collective, succeeds in evoking generalized visual, auditory, olfactory auras that the reader can fully share.

When we speak of "Pall Malls burning away on bureaus" or "buses hissing in the rainy streets" and "friends pinching roaches in the low light," we understand that the image is ours, that the poet is appealing to our experience as readers. The tone of the collective image can make even the most unique image seem to be a familiar one. While the poet often sacrifices the precision that comes from pinning his image down to specific time and space, the collective image can save a perception from obscurity, though it may be in itself obscure. The poet is, in a way, giving us part of his poem and hoping that our experience is broad enough to accept it.

9.

If this brief catalog does little to characterize student poetry or distinguish it sharply from any other poetry, maybe it at least suggests some bad habits which, in turn, have created a problem for us.

I think many college poets write under the heavy influence of intentionalism or author psychology, which most critics agree is a Romantic phenomenon. Instead of calculating specific poetic responses from our readers, instead of depending upon the crucial cognitive meanings of words, our writing process is much less measured. We have a strong conviction that the workings of our intricate psyches have rationales of their own and that the poetry we may produce spontaneously is justified by those often inscrutable rationales. Just as Wordsworth in his "Preface to the Lyrical Ballads" insisted that "my description of such objects as strongly excite those feelings will be found to carry along with them a purpose," we would like to say that our short poems, written between classes, contain their own inherent purposes; that, far from being the gags they sometimes read like, they are the profound manifestations of our psyches even though we may not be able to say exactly what the psychological or intentional origins of the poem and its meaning are. Perhaps, we deserve to have this faith. But I suspect that many are using their faith in the organizational abilities of their psyches to avoid organizing the poem on a conscious level. We may be using our own *imprecision voulue* as a crutch. We commit what Allen Tate calls "failures of connotation." By employing in our poems effusions of connotative words unattached to a central consciousness of what we are doing, we, in Tate's words, "yield a clutter of images that may be unified only if we forget the firm denotations of the terms."

10.

The introduction to the second *Alkahest* confesses: "I doubt if there are any Eliots published in these pages." This dumb expression of modesty actually contains a truth. The fact is that fewer and fewer of us do have it in them to become Eliots; few, in fact, would be able to recognize an Eliot in someone else. We are scanning the landscape for other things. Too often the carefully chosen word or assiduous poem goes by unnoticed. We admire the impeccable mind less and less, preferring the witty Brautigans in poetry and daring R. D. Laings in psychology. We are suspicious of the composed intelligence.

It is easy to be proud of this irreverence. Our politics, our style, our minds and our wits are sharpened by it. But, in respect to poetry, it may do us in. I simply don't think so many "serious" writers should fawn over Richard Brautigan. He is very good, but he is very unhealthy. He does not simply accommodate other media in his poetry; he turns poetry itself into another media. He encourages *poetic* failures. We must take more time to write our poems and eat our dinners. We have to be more careful. Some of us have been eating all-meat burgers for so long, we don't know what's good for us.

Hot Sausage Links:

An Allegory of American Politics

He studied the composition of foodstuffs, and knew exactly how many proteins and carbohydrates his body needed; and by scientific chewing he said that he tripled the value of all he ate, so that it cost him eleven cents a day. About the first of July, he would leave Chicago for his vacation, on foot; and when he struck the harvest fields he would set to work for two dollars and a half a day, and come home when he had another year's supply—a hundred and twenty-five dollars. That was the nearest approach to independence a man could make "under capitalism," he explained; he would never marry, for no sane man could allow himself to fall in love until after the revolution.

—Upton Sinclair, *The Jungle*

1.

Every time I eat Del Monte Royal Anne cherries in heavy syrup, I remember Estes Ranch in Colorado where, at the age of ten, I extravagantly ordered them for dessert and experienced the first and less damaging culinary disillusionment, The Quantity Crisis. I had been on horseback all day, and the strenuous activity had heightened in me the taste for something very cold and good. Despite a prohibitive price, I ordered Royal Anne cherries, fully expecting a bowl exactly equivalent in size to the depth of my desire for them. Instead,

I was brought a delicate glass cup with four Royal Anne cherries in heavy syrup. I will never forget it. Four cherries. Four sullen, light tan cherries in an ounce of juice. Quickly, I computed the injustice dealt me by figuring that I could have purchased two #2 cans of Royal Anne cherries in a grocery for the price of these four derelicts. Obviously, a serving of Royal Anne cherries such as this was intended only for those subliminal gourmets whose only satisfaction comes from *knowing* they have eaten Royal Anne cherries, and surely not from actually having eaten them, since eating four Royal Anne cherries is tantamount to eating none at all.

Too young to mount an effective protest, I quietly ate my dessert, shooting all four pits into the empty cup, and suffered in silence through my first culinary hurt. But far from being an isolated example, disappointments followed quickly and relentlessly; in Italian restaurants, meatballs were smaller and fewer than ever. Soda jerks served me ice cream sodas they had deviously managed to fill with a sugary foam and nothing else. Anxiously lifting the aluminum tops off dishes of Cantonese food, I was aghast at the size of the egg rolls. The long-awaited spareribs were either shriveled or fatty. Everywhere, my drinks were so generously endowed with crushed ice that my eager straw drained the cup in one sip. Bread baskets were emptied before orders were taken, never to be replenished. Was my expectation too great, my appetite too large, or even my eye for the slightest duplicity too acute?

The plot continued, and I construed it as a case of personal sabotage. Everywhere else I looked, kids were blissfully draining sixteen ounces of Orange Crush and were being supplied with far more chicken croquettes than they could consume. Or others proved more stoic and remained unflinching in the face of disastrously small scoops of Oregon blackberry. Did they have both good breeding and small appetites on their sides? It was only I whom the waitresses and chefs wished to outdo; they spent hours devising techniques to swindle and harass me, to leave me hungry. They contrived huge, but cunningly submerged, beds of shredded lettuce under my mound of guacamole, used false bottomed glasses, and had pictures in the menus which were totally misleading.

There was no end to the plot or to my indignance. But I was powerless before this conspiracy and came to view my own outbursts in cafés and requests that the waitress return my order to the kitchen for enlargement as mere formalities. The waitresses, I had to confess, were not at fault, and the chefs, also, soon escaped my condemnation. It was settled, then, beyond question and also beyond counterattack: I had no visible enemy, only the evidence of stunted meals. There was no one I could turn to, except perhaps to admit it was my fate to be forever short-changed.

First I sought to rectify matters by taking food from the plates of others. Actually, I started by shamelessly asking those I was eating with if I could have the remnants of their meals. It was, perhaps, an odd request but one, I found, to which there was only one possible response: if the article of food I had designated was, in fact, unwanted, its owner had no choice but to give it to me. Timing was difficult in the beginning, and I often made the mistake of asking for leftovers before they were left over. Misjudgments like this embarrassed the eater who was suddenly called upon to defend something which was already his, and it embarrassed me because it compounded my forgivable sin of appetite with unforgivable greed and boorishness. Worse, when the other finally did finish what he wanted and then offered me the remainder, I couldn't take it. I would grin foolishly, looking down at my polished plate, murmuring through my sauce-stained lips. I was hungrier than ever, but courteous enough to punish my own haste. Eventually, my timing became perfect, my technique impeccable, spiced with a quick humor that completely obscured my un-civility. And I was careful to eat out with light eaters whose appetites assured me of fulfillment.

I was soon awakened to the fact that asking others for their leftovers was hardly a revenge commensurate with the crimes perpetrated against me. I discovered the psychic and pabulatory (stolen goods somehow taste better) benefits of poaching eggs and stealing, in general, what my utensils and dexterity allowed me to. I became so selfish, so voraciously self-serving, that there was little that could prevent me from appropriating a desired object. Taking from friends' and strangers' plates alike, I was required to have sincere apologies ready in the event I was caught in the act. With strangers, I would look stupid and insensate and mutter something about kleptomania. With friends it was easier; a resonant laugh or elaborate story would serve.

Whether I was caught in the act or not, I was always apprehended shortly thereafter when the unsuspecting victim discovered the theft. His anger was usually aggravated by the fact that he was mad at himself for not having seen the crime take place beneath his nose. "Christ, you know I wanted the pickle!" he would scream. "My God, you always take the best part!" At these times, I usually assumed the role of a chastened criminal. You're right, I said sheepishly, that was really wrong. What did my pose really matter now that I had my food? At times, I was able to humor myself into absolution. If not, I remained the repentant criminal, ready to accept whatever just punishment was due; in most cases, a stern refusal to dine with me again.

When my fame had grown and I was reverently called the Fastest Fork in the South Cafeteria in high school, alerted schoolmates devised simple but effective defenses against my invasions. I was not surprised to find that kids on either side of me would hold one protective hand, palm down, over their trays as they ate. If I could not quickly and stealthily steal things from their unguarded trays, I was resigned to inactivity for that sitting. For, no matter how heinous I was, or was thought to be, I could not, in all good conscience, spear a friend's hand. My friends cheered this consideration and frequently rewarded me with gifts of olives, Fritos, and even half-sandwiches. For a while, sustained by payola, I did not go hungry.

Something happened then. It may have been an accidentally skewered hand, an overzealous theft, I don't recall, but I was banished to a small isolated table in the South Cafeteria for the rest of the year. I had a good friend who joined me there so I was not alone, but I was for the most part unfulfilled. The table was right by the door and, as an act of contempt and condescension, my former victims would, as they strode by my table on entering, fling tantalizing morsels of favorite foods in my direction. "Here you go," one would snicker and whip an Oreo against the wall behind me. I was hurt, but not mortally. I continued to function, resuming my food-filching outside of high school, startling elderly ladies into speechlessness at the Walgreen's lunch counter. When I became a senior, the underclassmen, whose small ears my dying legend had not failed to reach, would whisper to one another in my presence, and not without due respect, "there goes the Fastest Fork in the South Cafeteria." Noting them along the corridor walls, I would look slowly in their direction, swaggering, my pants pulled down almost to my pubic triangle, lift one succulent corner of my mouth, and strut on.

2.

There was, for instance, a Lithuanian who was a cattle butcher for the plant where Marija worked, which killed meat for canning only; and to hear this man describe the animals which came to his place would have been worthwhile for a Dante or a Zola. It seemed that they must have agencies all over the countries to hunt out old and crippled and diseased cattle to be canned. There were cattle which had been fed on "whiskey malt," the refuse of breweries, and had become what the men called "steerly"—which means covered with boils. It was a nasty job killing these, for when you plunged your knife

into them they would burst and splash foul-smelling stuff into
your face.
                              —Upton Sinclair, *The Jungle*

Beef, water, corn syrup, salt, dextrose, flavoring, sodium
erythorbate, sodium nitrite, sodium nitrate.
                              —Vienna, *Skinless Frankfurters*

Earlier this year, admits one tobacco executive, his company
"boosted the nicotine of most of our brands." The idea was to
"hook" smokers so that if advertising were to be banned entirely, the "need for a smoke" would keep people puffing.
                              —*Business Week*

I realized, not long after the demise of my career, or maybe
because of it, that there was a far more disturbing culinary
problem than the Quantity Crisis. There came to my attention another, a far more telling dilemma: the Quality Crisis.
Since the Quality Crisis first took the form of unsuspicious experiences of eating foods whose taste did not resemble what I
was accustomed to tasting, I understandably brushed the mis-
adventures aside. As quick as I was to discern behind my first
few Quantity Crises an entire plot directed solely at me, I
was equally as unwilling to see the plot that really did lie behind the first Quality Crises.
   Institutional cooking offered me my first opportunities to
ingest food whose flavor had been exchanged for another's. By
way of this kitchen alchemy, I was served fish which tasted like
fowl, fowl which tasted like meat, and meat reminiscent of
lyonnaise potatoes. At first, I was amused by the ingenuity of
the cooks and the innocence of my palate. In time, I ran
across what came to be called, by its victims, "mystery meat,"
a material so vague in form and elusive in taste that I could
only hastily eat it, hoping that its effects would not be more
offensive than its appearance. "Mystery meat" combined all
the less attractive attributes of other, identifiable dishes. It
came either in a mound on the plate (in which case the
mimeographed school menu insisted it was Salisbury steak) or

in slices (anything from veal to pork to roast beef). It was speckled with a confetti of white and muted yellow particles which gave the meat's surface an interesting, but inedible, complexion. Clinging tenaciously to the border was an amount of hardened, glistening fat which, because it could neither be separated from the meat nor be eaten with it, posed special problems. What difficulties that remained were concealed by a brownish fluid advertised as "pan gravy."

As I became inured to these diets, I looked upon them only as inconveniences, as enigmatic as logarithms were at the time, or the dim secrets of chemistry. When I was served inscrutable dishes which defied classification and digestion, I ate my fill. Who was I to argue? A crisis of quantity was something I could understand, hence something which enraged me. I was not being given enough; it hardly mattered what it was I was not being given enough of. But as long as I was eating sufficient quantities of food, its contents and its quality didn't faze me.

Besides, it was natural for me in high school to think that the world at large observed the same rules of ethics and quality that I obtained in my own home. As long as my mother prattled on about nutrition and balanced meals, her concern assured me of good food everywhere. Mollified by vague confidences in the world around me, I ate on, took in, and let out vast amounts of matter without wincing.

To what do I owe my sudden revelation that America Is Concealing the Facts about Her Food? To Julia Child, I believe, I owe much. Also to personal examinations of hot dogs and hamburgers, a simple test worth anyone's time. Perhaps those disquieting, almost imperceptible changes in my body spoke of hidden disaster. I became worried. The Crisis of Quality was far more insidious than the Crisis of Quantity. The former only suggested parsimony; the latter, unscrupulousness.

I am certainly not being poisoned outright, only polluted;

not ignored, but neglected. If meals aren't indigestible, they are usually unaesthetic. Menus turgid, the meals they describe, sparse and ugly. Where could I strike out? I could attack the rampancy of artificial foods or the uninventiveness with which all foods are prepared or the nutritional aspect (which I chose to let researchers and chemists handle) or packaging or hygiene. In my modest capacity as irate consumer (hardly crusader), I paid a visit to International Flavors and Fragrances in New York City where I sought the truth about artificial flavors and aromas.

As I boarded the bus on a gray (Misty Dawn) morning, I envisioned IFF as a small unkempt brick warehouse manned by disreputable scientists in stained aprons. They pored over vats, cauldrons, tureens, saucers, squirting pipettes full of essences and colors into already dense solutions. As they approached final solutions, they would clasp their hands together in anticipation of a new product which would flavor the ice creams, hard candies, and Shake 'N Bakes of this country. Unsanitary conditions, unwashed test tubes; there would be something almost agreeably illicit about the whole enterprise. As the bus scuttled across Manhattan, I wondered how hospitable they would be to a visitor. When I had called up earlier, a secretary had reluctantly agreed to let me come in Monday morning.

When the bus left me off, I stood in front of an immense an immaculate red brick building; the initials IFF were attached neatly to the wall in large chrome letters. No warehouse. I entered the air-conditioned factory and fingered my way along the index, selecting one of the five floors occupied by IFF. In the elevator, my preconceptions already shattered, I sensed an opposition so formidable, so well organized, so well paid and accredited that I quickly resigned myself to the reality that artificial flavors and fragrances were here to stay. Out of the elevator; the wall facing me was covered with Kodachromes of what looked like IFF's suburban plant. The parking lots were filled with large and powerful automobiles; the sky was contentedly blue. The pendulums of the lives of the employees swung happily from home to work and back again.

Before I even left my position in front of the Kodachromes and strolled toward the receptionist, I knew I was already deprived of my most intimidating weapon—that of preying on their insecurity. The simple truth was that IFF had no insecurities. Their factory was so well carpeted, well dusted, well maintained, and aromatic (Strawberry Welcome) that, regardless of their business, the operation had thrown around itself an impenetrable robe of shiny respectability. On the phone the previous Friday, I had interpreted the secretary's reluctance to receive me as surprise that anyone *wanted* to visit IFF and as unwillingness to entertain a guest at such a filthy place. I imagined her announcing afterwards to the employees, like a frenetic housewife on the eve of a big dinner party, that they would be having a guest on Monday and to be sure that everything was clean and in order by then. What, in fact, her reluctance conveyed was an annoyance at being disturbed by such an insignificant visitor, a mere student, with "a detailed and perverse interest in food." Beyond question, I was unwanted. Businessmen holding on to their frank brief cases were walking to and fro, their smiles bulging with promise, on their lips such phrases as "Bean Ecstasy" and "Cinnamon Moment." The gum they chewed, cracking on their molars, filled the pockets of air in front of their faces with sweet clouds of spearmint and licorice. I stood sheepishly as they passed, smelling faintly of Manhattan and the crosstown bus. They talked humorously, tersely, as they passed, saying things made funny only by their dullness. They stepped into the elevator, looking over their shoulders at me as if I were an unpalatable flavor. These were clearly men whose satisfied expressions indicated they possessed secrets beyond the reach of most mortals.

I offered no business, only curiosity. When my host asked me to sit down and snapped, "What's your line of business?" or "Whom do you represent?" was I going to respond by say-

ing, "I like food," a sentiment completely at odds with IFFs
basic sympathies? Although my cause, whatever it was, now
seemed deflated by the enterprise's classiness, I owed IFF
nothing, least of all mindless respect. Still, I remembered my
bad habit of being paralyzed by contact with the worst cases of
idiocy. Cowed by the whiteness of the walls (Spring Cauli-
flower) and a certain scented malevolence, my behavior was,
in the end, something less than outrageous, my actions less
disruptive than what the situation called for.

Pulling up my jeans, I took off toward the receptionist. At
the end of a winding plush corridor, I found her and across
from the desk a fountain, elaborately cut into the wall and
furnished with polyethylene ferns and rocks; the blue water,
trickling into a small pond, sounded like an old man perpetu-
ally tinkling in the next stall. I checked in, sat down, and
picked up a few pamphlets lined up on the coffee table. In
one titled *Fragrance*, I was instructed:

> Everyone likes a lift. Sometimes it's a new hat. Other times
> it is cooking a fancy new dish or going to a movie when you
> should really be home ironing clothes! One of the quickest
> and pleasantest lifts comes from putting on some perfume or
> splashing on some cologne. . . . Fragrance makes any job
> more pleasant, even washing dishes or filing correspondence.

Washing dishes and filing correspondence, I thought, are
surely two jobs one would never think that fragrance could
make more pleasant; there is no question that making phone
calls and raking leaves are two tasks easily enhanced by fragrances, but washing dishes and filing correspondences had
been, until this moment, in doubt. (The habit of mocking
and undermining advertising language and claims is, of course,
an easily acquired habit, decreasingly funny and fruitless. One
begins to wonder who reads ads without seeing through them.
Yet the same people for whom commercial claims are transparent somehow find political promises opaque and believable,
worthy of their vote or at least their renewed confidence in the
virtue of men.)

Fragrance should be part of good grooming, an essential step in getting dressed. No one today, even when alone, runs around without wearing lipstick or lip gloss—there is something naked about it. Perfume too makes you feel more dressed and more like you!

There is no goal to which this nation is more dedicated, and to which I am more dedicated, than to build a new structure of peace in the world where every nation including North Vietnam as well as South Vietnam can be free and independent with no fear of foreign aggression or domination.

—Richard Nixon

Why does this age, when dealing with most tenuous and suspicious propositions, strike the most absurd tone of certitude, as if the obscurity of a statement makes contradiction impossible?

So many people say, "After I do the dishes, I'll have a cigarette." Why not say, "I'll type that report and then put on some perfume."

A speech made in 1967 by the president of IFF ends:

. . . We believe we spend more than anyone else in the world on flavors and fragrance research. We want to share the results with you.

I was so consumed by the melodic religiosity of the speech that I could scarcely determine its subject matter; easily, the speech could have been about any product for which the public's need had not yet been fully cultivated and, hence, for which the product's promoters could create unspecified, sententious arguments. Bombs, amazing lighted pineapple centerpieces, tennis shoes, vaginal jellies: We want to share the results of this continuing effort with you.

It never occurs to certain industries to dismiss, even acknowledge, obvious objections as they leap over them, manufacturing self-justifying products. The need for artificial flavors and fragrances is a given, the question of motive slickly evaded, the idea of intent beside the point.

Let us, however, return to the war in Vietnam and the response that it has aroused among American intellectuals. A striking feature of the recent debate on Southeast Asian policy has been the distinction that is commonly drawn between "responsible criticism," on the one hand, and "sentimental" or "emotional" or "hysterical" criticism, on the other. . . . The "hysterical critics" are to be identified, apparently, by their irrational refusal to accept one fundamental political axiom, namely, that the United States has the right to extend its power and control without limit, insofar as is feasible. Responsible criticism does not challenge this assumption, but argues, rather, that we probably can't "get away with it" at this particular time and place. . . . Is the purity of American motives a matter that is beyond discussion, or is that irrelevant to discussion?

—Noam Chomsky, *American Power and the New Mandarins*

Although there are redeeming qualities to the artificial flavor and fragrance business, it is discussed as an utter inevitability, as though all lives depended on it, as though whole emaciated populations were crying out for "Mango Melon!" and "Tahitian Treat!" as though the peoples of the world, bored stiff with available essences, shrieked aloud together and clamored for new taco flavors.

I will ask Mr. F., our vice-president for flavor sales, to tell you something about flavors.

Mr. F: For the reasons that Mr. W. has mentioned we believe that companies like IFF with fragrance experience are best qualified to produce good flavor results. . . . I do not have to tell you gentlemen that flavor, like odor, is one of the important keys in bringing the customer back for those repeat sales that are needed to keep the product on the supermarket shelf.

It is not generally realized that the flavor business in the past five years has gone through a revolution. The fantastic instruments that are part of the technological fallout of the space age—the nuclear magnetic resonators, the high-resolution fast-

scan mass spectrometers, the radio isotopes, electron micro-
scopes, etcetera—enable us to take apart and put together
basic flavor components in a way impossible five years ago.
This information is most useful to our creative flavorists. We
can now produce imitation chicken, turkey, beef, pork, bacon,
mushroom, fish, fruit, and countless other flavors that will out-
perform the real thing in processed foods at the point of use.

A world has been created of which I am just not a part. Now,
perhaps IFF will begin to solve world food shortages: "We
could tell you how we think flavors will help unlock the riddle
of feeding more than twice today's world population, . . ."
but I simply can't accept IFF's a priori conviction that "since
General Foods has used imitation flavors for its Jell-O line for
years with excellent results," it must investigate all opportunities to use a facsimile of natural flavor and a recreation of natural scent.

We hope you will send some of your people to visit us here
at IFF on Fifty-seventh Street and let us take them through
our laboratories.
Thank you all for coming.

Mr. C. was rotund, in a white shirt and congenial mood. It
wasn't long after he had led me into his stark white office that
I realized there was no hope that he was going to take me
through their laboratories. He adopted an air of jovial secrecy
from the beginning: "Certainly I would like to let you see our
laboratories, but I'm afraid it's just not our policy at the moment."

I started, "I'd simply like to know a few things about artificial flavors and fragrances." He stopped me there with a smiling "First you must understand that most artificial flavors contain a degree of natural flavor too. Only the WONFs are
purely artificial."
"WONF?"
"Without natural flavor."
"Oh," I said, as I was to say often in the next half hour. It

was clear the burden of questioning was on my shoulders, but I was without questions. Mr. C. sat calmly behind his desk, his chubby hands clasped behind his neck. I sat in the windowless white office, in his odorless air, wanting more than anything else to ask him a question so embarrassing, so penetrating, so ethically powerful that it would force him to sit up suddenly, cough nervously into his fist, and gather together all the moral defenses he had. He would then try to defend himself and his business, but I would catch him with a riposte so stunning that he would sink into his chair, defeated. I had grown to love Fancy Fruits and Orange Julius, but they suddenly became odious, and I would have sacrificed all future contact with them just to call into question for a moment, quoting obscure but accurate statistics, the whole nature of IFF.

"Uh, how many artificial flavors do you have?" I asked.

"I'm really not sure," Mr. C. replied, smiling.

"Oh," I said. I, too, clasped my hands behind my head and scanned the white room with my eyes, as if the next question was scrawled minutely somewhere on the walls.

"Tell me," I intoned matter-of-factly, "about how much flavoring do you use, on the whole, in a food."

"Well," Mr. C. replied, smiling, his hands clasped behind his head, "we use a surprisingly small amount."

"Oh," I remarked casually.

"Often," Mr. C. saved me, "no more than half an ounce for one hundred pounds."

"Half an ounce for a hundred pounds," I said.

"Yes," Mr. C. replied.

"And how old is IFF now?" I asked.

"Well," Mr. C. replied, "as such IFF is twelve years old, that is, after amalgamation. We do have branches in twenty-nine foreign countries around the world."

"Twenty-nine foreign countries," I observed. So, I thought, you have the gall to flavor and deodorize twenty-nine foreign countries. Quickly I wondered if I could pull it off, if I could say it right out loud. "Now come on, Mr. C., let's face up to facts. You're in an unethical business. Your insistent use of artificial and imitation flavors and fragrances, a use I might add which you feel you have the right to spread all over the globe, is killing natural flavors and fragrances. In the name of large profits, you are putting unadulterated and beneficial natural flavors and fragrances right out of business. Now, I know that artificial flavors and fragrances sell more products, and might in the end help to alleviate world hunger by transforming vegetable protein, yeasts, and natural carbon resources into food, and I know that you can't do anything about the farmers who are paid millions of dollars each year to destroy their natural crops, and I know that the enormous volumes of food needed today necessitates the use of artificially manufactured flavors, but don't you see that the growth of your industry all but eliminates efforts to work extensively with natural crops. The steps you are taking should be the last ones taken, after natural resources are exhausted. If we weren't destroying sea life off every coast, burning our own surplus food, spraying our crops with pesticides, we wouldn't need you. You've created an artificial olfactory environment without ever having noticed the natural one. And then there's the aesthetic aspect . . ."

"Tell me," I asked Mr. C. "How do you go about testing your flavors?"

"Well," Mr. C. replied, removing his hands from his neck and laying them like two moist pink fish on the deck, "we have professional tasters and smellers or, more precisely, if you will, an Expert Board and an Experience Board that hold test panels daily." He chose his sentences as if they were ball points in his breast pocket.

Then, taking the initiative for the first time, he took out a periodical called *Food Product Development*. "Let's take a look at this," he said warmly. As he leafed through, we passed ads concerning ethyl vanillin, *Another imitation cinnamon?*, a recipe for stifado from the Middle East, and a picture of a

bowl of beef stew next to which the copy read: "This dish was
made with fresh vegetable and beef-flavor chunks of TVP
textured vegetable protein. You could also include meat. . . ."
"*Maltrin:* It's clear, it's tasteless, it's viscous, its uniform."

As we passed an ad for a fruit product, Mr. C. looked up at
me and said with alacrity, "Berry flavors are in big demand."

I shook my head knowingly. He flipped a few more pages,
stopping at a color photograph of brussels sprouts in a bowl.
"It doesn't look like they did too much to this broccoli," Mr.
C. said. "Maybe just added a little butter."

When Mr. C. showed me out, I expected him to press a
new exciting kind of mint in my hand or a variety of smoked
meat. But I left empty-handed and, as I had expected, disturbed by the illness of large institutions. Ostensibly a smooth-
functioning and profitable corporation, IFF was still a world
in itself and, like a sequestered asylum whose inmates live together peaceably by using their own moral code, justified its
actions only in terms of IFF. Whether IFF did or did not
commit a certain act depended on its feasibility in the context
of the artificial flavor and fragrance business. Larger issues calling into question the nature of the whole industry or the
ethical advisability of widespread use of imitation flavors and
fragrances when so much could be done to salvage the real
thing from pollution, destruction, and misuse seemed to be
outside the realm of IFFs interests. After all, can one expect
IFF to be concerned with theoretical matters when it has to
struggle with clients and employees and the problems of daily
business? This is what saddened me as I got out of the elevator: Any large enterprise sacrifices a broad perspective as soon
as it becomes bureaucratized and, in the process, loses many
ethical and aesthetic considerations amidst the debris of its
operation. The individual human enterprise suffers the same
history. As it becomes cluttered with necessities irrelevant to
the act of living, it gradually forgets its obligations to itself: to
suspect anything that interferes with the course of its perfec-

tion, to suspect rules that precede the act, to condemn any system that obscures the details it concerns.

I was a "hysterical critic," refusing to accept the fundamental axiom of IFFs life, that, indeed, polysorbate 60 had to appear in my kosher food, that the extant United States Government is its own excuse for being.

I could not denounce IFF categorically. But when its work was aesthetically pleasing, it hardly seemed ethically just. When the use of imitation products seemed inevitable, the products themselves were offensive. But I was powerless again, dull; when I should have been outrageous, I was quiet, even exuding that kind of intelligent curiosity that made Mr. C. feel too much at ease.

There was no wheat here, no corn, no fields, no small pieces of rye bread crust littered on the floor, no small path leading to a garden through green and overgrown trees, no one even spitting up disagreeable matter into his handkerchief. Even the relationships were expedient, the duplistic ententes of an airline stewardess and her lecherous passenger in which both are free to reveal themselves as they like, to make erotic promises, since the end of the flight effectively ends their relationship. Contact in which the stewardess, aware of what is both permissible and victorious, slyly uncovers some moist sexual aspect which she promptly withdraws from under the nose of the junior executive, replacing it with a dinner tray. What lasts? Once off the plane or out of the office, one is absolved of responsibility.

I could not protest to Mr. C.; we were too far apart. Mr. C.'s careful explanations, his examples, were all based on presuppositions I had never agreed to support. He, on the other hand, had taken my acceptance of them for granted. I had left him far behind; or he had left me behind. Whichever, I listened to what he said as if it were only purely hypothetical discourse and not the insane reality of his life.

I wanted to destroy his premises. But if one is confronted with a murderer, one doesn't appeal to him by trying to dem-

onstrate that a life of crime is bad. One should simply barter
instead for his own life. I did neither; on the bus, I sat at the
rear, my scalp drawing tight around my skull, my hands, motionless and damp, in my lap.

3.

At the bottom are the so-called gravy mixes. They are simply preparations of the previous sort, adapted to instant use. I
place them at the bottom, not because they taste so much
worse [than homemade gravies], but because they do more
harm. They confirm our bondage to the commercial taste by
making it easier to achieve than any other. They insure the
continued progress of American cooking toward institutional-
ism. Two more generations of instant gravy eaters and no one
will remember what a domestic kitchen smelled like. Men
will be able to walk into a hospital at dinnertime . . . and,
wonder of wonders, think fondly of Mother.
                            —Father Capon, *Supper of the Lamb*

It all took place on two immense floors, the first and the
second. So big that they were partitioned into smaller rooms
and aisles by flimsy Bainbridge board walls that extended
halfway up to the ceiling. The walls were cream or light beige,
and far away. The atmosphere was suffused with a variety of
odors, coming from different displays; the smell of bean
sprouts and Wesson Oil attracted me to one corner of the
room, to an exhibit of Flavos shrimp egg rolls. Shrimply Delicious. A crowd, maybe fifteen or twenty people, men with
straw hats on the bands of which the different names of products were printed, leaned over one another to get a look into
the aluminum trays where the hostess was placing the newly
fried shrimp rolls and getting everybody to touch the objects
whose grease had already saturated the Scott towel. Even as
she placed the shrimp rolls side by side in the tray, the hostess
began, in that geometric tone that somehow attempts to lend
pliability to memorized lines, ". . . And [they are forever
starting sentences with *and*] these Flavos shrimp rolls are

fresh-frozen daily in one of our five plants in the area. As you will be able to tell by tasting, we have combined the crispness . . ."

A few years ago, a friend and I first ran across shrimp rolls in Providence where a mobile snack bar stopped on a corner every night. When we each finally ordered one, the guy looked querulously at us, dug his hand into a freezer, and pulled up two pallid batons of dough flecked with ice. He deep-fried them in fat and delivered them to us in thin wax-paper envelopes with a picture of a smiling Chinaman and a review of the envelope's contents, such as It's Deelicious or Try One Now! We ate them voraciously, craning our necks forward in front of our bodies so that the grease dripped on the sidewalk. Because of our infatuation at that time with the possibilities of genitalic metaphor, we dubbed them Pookie Burgers and came back from then on a few nights a week to eat them, so crisp on the outside and soft on the inside. We began to enjoy them immensely, enjoy the grease and the leafy stuffing, enjoy the way we ate them, standing on the cold sidewalk on the corner in the middle of February.

Of course, I couldn't bear to even look at them in the tray, the aluminum tray, in the fluorescent light, with all the men and women pinching them between their thumbs and forefingers and saying "It's delicious" and "Why don't you try one, Bernice." I realized that I had been eating, not Pookie Burgers, but the idea of eating Pookie Burgers on the streets of Providence. Yet these men wolfing the shrimp rolls kept coming back for more, raving about the duck sauce. Who were these men?

These men were there to do business. They were all good men and wore Corfam shoes. Many of them would have worn sneakers, but no one nowadays does good business in tennis shoes. So they wore Corfam shoes and dark suits which made sharp turns at the shoulder and which caressed the torso, which were snug at the waist but let out just below and didn't pull at the crotch. Their pant legs fell lazily down at an ample cuff which, in turn, fell wide and luxuriously over their shoes. They wore shirts and ties which were very colorful, and which were meant to be observed and remarked upon as being colorful. Their hair was shaped neatly behind the ears, lower than last year, long on the neck, shiny and with body.

I know adults who raise interesting children and live in intriguing houses who write at the bottom of thank-you notes to liberal friends who have sent them get-well presents and birthday gifts, Fuck Nixon. And many of these men were there. And I know men with stickers on their cars supporting peace and ecological action, who took time off from work to canvas in their neighborhoods and where they work, and many of these men were there. I know men like those that the two nineteen-year-old girls who sat at the Fulton Packing Company desk all day described to me: "You know they're hanging around and you know they're there and they've been undressing you with their eyes all day and finally they come up to you like they're going to ask you about cold food storage and then they touch you in places that are close to the E zones, but so no one can see, and they say 'Honey, you know a girl like you could make a mint tonight, if you wanted to' and then they say 'think about it' and walk away."

I know that many of these men were there, too, and that many of them were the same men with the interesting kids and the time to spend in radical action. They were men who read good books on the weekends and contemplatively drink Scotch in the afternoon, but who smash their business friends in the gut while they're eating shrimp rolls and bellow: "Hey, you fucking son of a bitch! How are you."

This was not the Wisconsin State Fair, but it almost was. It was the Forty-Fifth Annual New England Hotel–Motel and Restaurant Show at Hynes Auditorium in Boston. On my shirt, a lady at a typewriter had pinned a piece of green paper enclosed in a plastic cover which said as much.

Before I arrived at the convention hall, I was already armed with evidence of and complaints against the food conspiracy. Beyond doubt, I was well-fed, but only because I was the victim of a conspiracy that guaranteed facial glow and internal corruption. To all the eager purchasers and dealers whose products my rosy complexion attested to, it looked as if I had no reason to complain. Regardless of what I already felt, I didn't know at the time I entered the convention how much more I could learn to feel. It was as though I was about to enter the Pentagon, certain that no contact with the real thing could possibly augment my political radicalism, only to learn the interminable illness of what was going on, only to be convinced that the real thing was actually worse than the reports hovering around it.

Yet I found much to like. Perhaps what I liked was the perverse joy I derived from such an exposition of bad taste and deception. Perhaps it was the perversity itself, perhaps I like the concept of food too much to be revulsed by the most egregious abuse of it. In any case, I was so entranced by the Forty-Fifth New England Hotel–Motel and Restaurant Show that I did not leave until it closed at 5 P.M.

I walked directly to a large area of the floor which contained the Epicurean Club of Boston exhibit. "The annual Salon of Culinary Art is the chef's 'art gallery,' the one place where he can give full rein to his artistry and imagination, where his most creative achievements can be displayed in all their. . . ." The first thing I noticed was a display of prepared potato dishes, arranged in forty white dishes on a white tablecloth. There were eight kinds of deep-fried potatoes: sliced, diced, hashed; grated, waffled; whipped, whole, and chipped; each garnished with a twig of parsley. Next to these were eight dishes of boiled-in-the-peel potatoes: whipped, waffled; hashed, whole, and diced; sliced, grated, and chipped, and eight parboiled potatoes done up in the very same way. Then they took eight miscellaneous potatoes and unto them hashed, diced, gassed, wholed; sliced, whipped, chipped; and grated.

On the table next to the potatoes, some chef had taken

liberties with carrots, zucchini, tomatoes, onions, and peppers,
stuffing them lengthwise with mushrooms, potatoes, spinach,
carrots, tomatoes, zucchini, olives; widthwise, with carrots,
onions, zucchini, pepper, squash, turnips; otherwise, with
asparagus, chickpeas, kohlrabies, and hot peppers; slit them
and glazed them, stuffed them backwards and forwards, on
their backs and on their knees, glazed them, sauced them,
skinned them, and arranged them on the table in eight rows
of eight.

One of the many numerous tallow sculptures in the exhibit
was a white hand, three feet tall, in the position of the peace
sign. Like an ice creation at a winter carnival, it rose majesti-
cally from its doilied cloth. It was titled, "Give Peace a
Chance." The motif was sustained by the dove of peace, a
prepared dove on its back on a silver platter, fringed with
pimientos and spearmint leaves, its thin charred feet jutting
up into the air, its frightened head, perspiring with glaze,
resting to one side.

Moving on. A display called "Hold Your Tongue." A platter
of six beef tongues, inlaid with a mosaic of enameled mushrooms and olives in the shapes of crocuses. Two of the dark
brown, luculent tongues were decorated as boats, two as shoes,
and two as small forest animals; all the details done in pastel-
colored frosting. There were turkeys glazed inedible, like
large marzipan candies, flounders surrounded by bread boats
cargoed with caviar and shrimp, crown of lamb DuBarry
sprinkled with crushed gold chips.

Can't stop now: galantine of capon, covered with gelatin,
feet encased in paper booties, mousse of fillet of sole Waleska,
and lobster Parisienne, a dour crustacean sporting a thick bro-
cade of aspic in which were set pimientos and anchovies cut
in the shapes of hearts, spades, diamonds, and clubs. There
were pastries of all conceivable colors and walks of life, green
and pink, made to look like books and boats and houses and
lambs and basketball courts and crucifixes and nativity scenes.
The Henry Peabody Regional Vocational School had a large

table or two to itself, one of which supported an edible facsimile of the school. The instructor of the school, whose exhibits spread around him like a miniature domain, explained
to a visitor: "Look, it's the last day of the show. And anyway
the reason the show only lasts three days is for the benefit of
the Culinary Art Show whose exhibits are about gone by now.
Look at that one over there, the watermelon is all shriveled.
As a matter of fact, you can see that almost all the melon balls
are just about gone. Hell, how do you expect any cake as large
as this one to stand up for three days?"

Off to the left, a coconut rabbit, with shredded coconut and
surrounded by a half dozen rabbit tongues standing on end,
curling inward toward the center of the platter.

This was the Culinary Art Salon. It was impressive, but a
person could starve. Like painters who lather their canvases
with reckless tubes of oils, these chefs attempted to arrive at
art through opulence and spectacle. And, in fact, they succeeded because they made little pretense of preserving their
medium in the process. The displays were so extravagantly
engineered and embellished that they no longer needed to be
made of edible material. The process had happily overtaken
the substance.

Elsewhere, the odor of Convention was so strong that it
overwhelmed its subject, with less fortunate results. With little respect for food, Convention had taken over, denouncing
what taste and justice seemed possible in favor of grandeur and
efficiency, just as it had taken over these men, so well behaved
and laconic elsewhere, but so beefy and clownish here.

I picked up a pamphlet. What's new with Instant Potatoes?
it asked excitedly. The words *sales bulletin* were written in the
midst of a galaxy of stars. Instant Breakthrough. Extra Rich
came spewing out of a spud no longer able to contain its fabu-
lous secret . . . Complete Potato Pearls. New, convenient
pack, specially developed for the foodservice industry. Six 3½
lb. bags to a case and each bag contains 100 servings—just
enough to fill a full-size 4" steam pan.

Whitatos.

I raced past Convenient Food Systems and Magic Shakes. Leering men slick with Crisco held out finger sandwiches and dishes of turkey à la king. I was suddenly lost and dizzy, in a movie whose sordid images had been contrived by someone other than myself. I remembered Sartre in the movies when he was a child: "End of Part I. The lights would go on, it was a sudden awakening. Where was I? In a school? In an official building? . . . Confused murmurs filled the hall, language was reinvented, the usherette would walk up and down selling hard candies." I was awakened to a rush of purchasers and manufacturers; no one looked familiar; coated black rabbit tongues darted in and out of their mouths, their lips were lined with thin veins. I reached for a cup of Kultured Klam Chowder and nervously fingered the bowl of oyster crackers, popping them into my mouth like Sen-Sen. The juke in the corner began to play "Green Eyes," "Green, Green Grass of Home," "Star Dust," "Misty." Guffawing men brushed past me, some had cocktail sauce on their shirts; others, creamed spinach. A man dressed in cowboy clothes passed. He wore a black Western-cut jacket with heavy white stitching, an embroidered white shirt, and a thin tie. He stopped, perhaps aware of our mutual oddity.

"Helluva show," he said. "Hey, see these sideburns? I wear em long so's I can feel like you young people. Pretty good idea, huh! Hey, if you really want something good, get on over to Private Prince Pizza."

From a corner of the room: "Girls, they'll think you spent all night long making these fancy cuts. But it only takes you a few minutes, girls. The knife is dish-water safe. The handle is Dinex, by Dupont. Now let's test this blade's sharpness, not by cutting something hard like a bone or a frozen steak; no sir, girls, you know as well as me that the true test of this knife's sharpness is its ability to cut through this ripe tomato! Just look at that!"

Here were large square chrome machines which did nothing

all day but dispense to visitors creamy doses of its contents.
Hostesses in trim uniforms offered rolled slices of head cheese
and olive and pimiento loaf to me.

"You know, girls," she said, sweeping the vegetables
through the hole in her wood cutting board, "you know,"
she said, cropping her words neatly at the end, "you take your
butcher's knife, probably the sharpest thing you have in the
house. . . ."

Not far away, near the simulated bar at which a man in a
body shirt demonstrated ice crushers and pressurized soda
systems, the interior of an office had been created. I joined
the crowd gathering there for the psychodramas presented
every half hour.

A young executive with a mike around his neck was dialing
feverishly at a telephone. With exaggerated sighs, he successfully conveyed his frustration, while his secretary at the desk
asked, "What's wrong, Mr. Brown?"

"Darn these telephones!" he exclaimed, banging the re-
ceiver down. "I've been trying to get an outside line for ten
minutes." More people drifted toward the group to watch.

"I'm sorry," the secretary replied, adjusting her mike and
batting her eyes.

"But this is a very important phone call and I have to get in
touch with Mr. Cummings before he leaves the office in five
minutes."

"I don't know what I can do, Mr. Brown," she said. "This
is such an antiquated phone system."

"Miss Hartley," pleaded Mr. Brown. "There must be something you can do. I must get through."

"Gee, but, I . . ."

"Obviously," Mr. Brown said confidentially to the audience,
turning away from Miss Hartley, "she hasn't heard of Norelco
Phone Systems, the most dramatically modern and advanced
phone system available today. With Norelco Phone Systems
Programs, there won't be any fretting, there won't be any
waiting. All your calls are placed instantly and automatically."

More people arrived, carrying shrimp rolls and Pepsis. When the crowd quieted down, the young executive was again standing in front of the secretary's desk, their mikes in place. "I'm leaving this instant, Miss Carter," he said.

"I'm sorry, Mr. Bentley," she said, "but I can't possibly have your bill ready before you leave for the airport."

Sam Rosseppi, cook for the Harvard Club of Boston, stood in the corner in his old tweed overcoat, seething on a nubbin of fish fillet. He watched a cardboard display of a chef with a mechanical arm that went up and down, holding the message Good and Good for You. Two young girls passed him, their short skirts hiked up to their quails, and he shook his head, slowly, from side to side.

Ahead, a mannequin. A long-legged, round-faced mannequin, propped up against a railing near the Corningware exhibit. Wore a powder blue matching skirt and short-sleeved sweater, stacked heels. An excellent mannequin because the light on its legs modulated from light to dark around the calf; on most mannequins, the play of the light on the limbs is very hard, never hiding the fact that they are plaster or plastic. But this mannequin had a suppleness. Even the breasts were rounded, falling slightly as they seemed to respond to gravity, not like most mannequin tits which point due north as though shot stiff with silicon. Although the mannequin had evidently been made with some new lifelike material, the hands were still stiff and textureless, the tips painted bright red. Still, as I moved closer, I averted my eyes as if the mannequin were real, as if it might suddenly look in my direction. As I approached, I pretended I was surveying the displays to my right. I didn't look close enough to see that there were no black lines at the elbows where the upper and lower arms are usually joined together or that the forehead was discolored by a scaly rash of pimples under the make-up. It was only as I passed her, my eyes on the floor, that I stopped, seeing a faint blue vein on her ankle.

"I get to rest now anyhow," she said, to no one in particular. "Yeech! This goddamn make-up is so hot." She smoothed an eyelash back in place. "Thank God I only do this for fifteen. Got fifteen off. Got a light?"

"Who you work for?" I asked, as the smell of acetate rose from between her legs.

"Them," she pointed behind her. "They pay me well; it's not bad."

"What do they do?" I asked.

"Hell if I know. They don't pay me to know anything. They pay me to look pretty without moving a muscle."

"And you really attract people?" I asked.

"Look at you buddy."

"You're probably the best advertising they've got."

"Not exactly," she said, "There's him too." She pointed across the aisle to a dashing male mannequin in a sharkskin suit.

"Nice meeting you," I said after that short pause which permits you to say nice meeting you without a transition.

"Yeah," she said, licking a bit of curd off the corner of her mouth. "Nice meeting you."

"This is sick," I told the lady who was demonstrating fresh-frozen omelettes. She took a waxed carton of prepared eggs and ingredients which remains frozen until use and spilled some of its contents onto the grill to create a perfect omelette.

"Why?" she asked.

"Don't you understand that this is going to be an unbelievably popular product and every woman will have one in her freezer and in ten years, no one will know what an egg is?"

"But," she protested, "this is a convenience food for institutions. Here, try one with mushrooms."

"But what's to stop anybody from buying the product?" I pleaded. "Look. An omelette is a challenge. Everyone in life should strive to make a good omelette. But you have just taken that challenge away for ever. It's sick."

"How did you like the mushroom one?" she asked irritably.
"You'll excuse me now, but I have to show these people the
product."

"Lady!" I cried. "Let these people make their own omelettes!"

"Shhh," she glared at me.

"C'mon kid," a lady who was watching said. "Get lost."

"Lady," I whispered, "they need your omelettes like they
need somebody to wipe themselves."

"Sir, are you going to quiet down or am I going to have
call a guard?"

I hesitated, looking around at the growing crowd of people
waiting anxiously for the demonstration to continue. I looked
up at the great white ceiling of the convention hall. "I think
I'll quiet down," I said.

"Girls, you see this little indentation at the end of the knife?
Well, this is a handy little extra we call the roast beef pick-up."

If one could hope to live one's entire life without being, in
some crucial way, effected by those untouchable lunchers who
make our Whitatos as well as our national policies, I would
not have to spend time occasionally convincing myself that I
possess my own destiny. But we are all living, everyday, in a
convention hall, consuming promising products which, once
safely installed in our systems, are free to assault our bodies
and minds from that most advantageous interior position. I
can hear the shrimp rolls conspiring within me. They speak in
a hushed tone at night, awakening me with their murmurous
oaths. As for the unaccountable volumes of trash that I am
served by elected officials, and which I for so long obligingly
ate, all that too lives inside of me, working day and night to
weaken my resistance. Surely, they have succeeded, for I
catch myself lingering too long at the convention, I find myself turning on the television to the president on Tuesday

night, I find myself really eating Whitatos when I am hungry and there is nothing else.

The truth is that this world is not mine. The indications that I am in foreign territory are not flagrant; entire days go by and I may not notice any of the warnings. The indications are too often subtle, inscribed in the face of the Kultured Klam Man. Sometimes I even find them on myself, like fleas. Even when so many of them are conveniently amassed at a convention, they are easily mistaken for something else.

All these things have been said before. We know what it is like. We know that the Dinex handles will detach themselves from the blade after two weeks, and we will attribute the occurrence to the general order of things. The guy who sticks me in the mouth with a shrimp roll is, at the same time, stabbing me in the back with something far more distasteful. We know this.

But why should we be surrounded with degrading objects? Is it without cause that I am suspicious of these small details? There is a decadence that escapes the eye, that has such an air of tentativeness (conventions close after a week, the troops are withdrawn for a moment) that sometimes I refuse to take it all seriously.

In fact, I continue to suck Softee cones and abide by some national policies, a practice which leaves me in a more precarious position than I can imagine. So I must learn to accompany my aesthetic protests and pledges of austerity with a purge of my own guilts. But sometimes that's the hardest thing in the world, to turn down a shrimp roll late at night in the middle of winter in Providence, Rhode Island.

One Entrecôte To Go,
Easy on the Beárnaise:
Food as People's Art

1.

Food is more important than poetry.
— W. H. Auden, *Esquire*, January 1970

Although I know I am taking unfair advantage of its impli-
cation, I attribute to Auden's statement a judgment of food
based on more than biological necessity. Auden, surely, is
also speaking of the aesthetic possibility of gastronomy; of the
question of choice involved in cooking; of color and texture;
of the chromatic and compositional problems of preparing a
meal, of arranging a plate. Auden's statement betrays an
artist's eye for the forms of the physical world as well as a
sensitive palate.

What is concealed in the quote is an exaltation of food as
a visual, tactile, plastic, colorful art form. However, because
food is also so functional, its aesthetic qualities are often
overlooked. Edibility, food's singular characteristic which
tends to divert our attention from its artistic nature, is precisely the element which makes it a unique, almost complete,
art form.

Edibility. In the end, we consume the creation, take it into
our own body. Its edibility not only brings us closer to the

work by eliminating awkward distances between, for instance, the painter and viewer or poet and reader, but the ability to internalize the object (meal) places us in a position to be seriously, viscerally, even gastro-intestinally, affected by it.

Imagine crumpling up the pages of *The Wasteland* into small paper balls which, when digested with all their allusions and multilingual density, might produce cramps as a sign of incomprehensibility or, on the other hand, that satiety which designates good literature. Unfortunately, most of our reactions are not formed so spontaneously. We are kept from many objects of art by our own intellectual apparatus and insistence on explaining the complexities of creation. It has become harder and harder for us to be intimate with our art. When we look at a painting, even the closest scrutiny may leave us cold. Something as trivial as a stuffed nose may keep us from enjoying a trip to the museum. For reasons irrelevant to the appreciation of art, the impact of a whole gallery may elude us. We can envision ourselves, under certain circumstances, mistaking a bad poem for a much better one. Yet I doubt sincerely whether the most severe stultification of the senses would prevent one from protesting a bad meal.

But far more immovable than physical and temperamental obstacles to the apprehension of most art forms is our own intellect. In literature, art, and to a lesser extent, music, the reacting human mind, even at peaks of receptiveness, often confuses intellectual and emotive responses.

Take *Icarus* by Breughel, for instance (Auden did). Do we like it for its mythological content or for its rendering of the scene or for what mixture of the two? Do we like it because we are able to tell our museum date some background information about it or because there is something ineffably beautiful about the green waves? Our familiarity with art history or Edith Hamilton's *Mythology* may get in the way of our aesthetic vision.

Our ability to extricate the emotive/aesthetic response from the intellectual/academic response is hampered particularly in dealing with literature where the words on the page have a life of their own, although they purport to stand for something else. Needless to say, the aesthetician is almost dispensable today, even obsolete, in the verbal disciplines. Critic W. K. Wimsatt states rather bluntly: "The intellectual character of language makes literature difficult for the aesthetician." Or, as Marshall McLuhan put it, the spoken word "is the extension of man in speech that enables the intellect to detach itself from the vastly wider reality." If this point needs elaboration, it would be wise simply to look at some college students' textual analyses to see how many students are technicians for whom a judgment of taste or pure form requires nonanalytic tools we have forgotten how to use.

Instilled by our education with a reverence for content before form, for a point of view before total sensory appraisal, we tend to confront even the most visual, affective arts with an analytic mentality. For months after Picasso's enigmatic fifty-foot sculpture was uncovered in a downtown Chicago plaza, discussion centered frantically on whether it was a woman, a dog, or a bird. Newspapers covered the controversy greedily, and it wasn't until people finally felt they could identify it that they were able to react. When Dylan Thomas spoke at MIT in 1953, his lyrically eccentric speech was met with silence by an audience of what must have been tight-lipped students and professors who seemed incredulous that a great poet could deliver a talk that was witty, ingenious blasphemy, a verbal texture, and nothing else. Misdirected arguments over the *nouvelle vague* in cinema, for a last example, almost constitute an affront to the cinematic art. It is no wonder some of us cannot distinguish between a smoky link and a knish.

Yet happily, most of us can, for food is one art which we don't, and can't, overintellectualize. Because we transfer our reactive mechanism from the mind/eye to the eye/nose/stomach/soul, our appreciation of the art is diminished by neither an inferior education nor a weak mind. There is room for the neophyte gourmet, the connoisseur, the glutton, the macrobiotic, the fat and the lean.

It would be foolish to suggest that food can be interpreted and enjoyed equally by everyone; it does require a knowledge of cooking, a cultivation of the palate, and less frequently, a durability of the system. But certainly there are fewer obstacles to the attainment of delicate taste buds than there are in the way of good literary, musical, or artistic critical faculties.

Food has good politics. And food, unlike all other arts, is close to being completely investigable to all. We can press our thumb through the skin of an orange and break it apart; smell it, taste it, hear it, use it, squeeze it, chew it, digest it, decompose it, excrete it, put it against our foreheads on hot days and in our pockets on the way to a show. We possess it like no other art. It doesn't conceal its etymology quite as completely. The orange is nonfigurative, nonmetaphorical. The orange stands for itself; it is its own metaphor.

Another advantage to the art of food is the proximity of creation to public consumption. Usually, a meal is observed and eaten soon after it is prepared. Other works of art may not be brought to their public for months and years, a fact which doesn't automatically diminish them, but one which allows, in the intervening period of time, critics and changing perspective almost to transform them into something that they were not at their moment of creation. With food, the object is delivered immediately and entirely to its audience.

The sooner we acknowledge that both the preparation and the consumption of food are legitimate art forms, the sooner we may all recapture the innocent and life-giving delights of cooking and eating.

2.

That is a thing you can't get in a chophouse—I mean: a spiced beef in which the jelly does not taste of glue and the beef has caught the flavor of the carrot.
—Marcel Proust, *In a Budding Grove*

Zum Zum is out; the Varsity Spa is in. Hostess cupcakes are out; green salads with minced clams are in. Eating with only utensils is out; using hands and other foods to eat with is in. Spooning plain yogurt into half an avocado is in, as is wheat germ, which always has been; veal cutlets which look like wallets are out. Putting Wheatena in your mouth is out; putting it on your mouth is in.

Eating out is in; eating in is in. Eating your meal on the table is out and in; eating it on the floor is in and out. Eating in dim light is, and has been, preferable to eating in strong light, but then eating in the sunshine is better than in dark rooms. Rooms with white walls, starkly furnished, enhance a meal as does summer or extreme cold, and oddly, rooms crowded with numerous small objects also create favorable atmospheres.

The ambience one eats in, like the gallery or the auditorium or the special privacy one likes to read in, is an inextricable part of the eating experience. Ambience, more so than food itself, is cheap, obeying a peculiar law which says that the earthiest, most honest atmospheres are found in some of the cheapest restaurants. Many people believe otherwise and pay for their innocence. Just as many artists and their agents capitalize on an easily influenced, indiscriminate public and sell at exorbitant prices undercooked works of art, so do many costly restaurants, dealing in an elegance disembodied from their product, victimize a public constantly confusing obsequious waiters with good food.

Ambience should never try to conceal the quality of the food, although it can enhance the enjoyment of a fair meal. Like Mount Rushmore, a work of art whose significance and craftsmanship is somehow improved by its debt to the environment, many inexpensive restaurants overcome an unexceptional menu with an alchemizing atmosphere.

The art of food is a total effect, localizing itself in the mouth and stomach. We digest not only the dish but the feeling of being in the room and among the people around us. For this reason, if one is eating out inexpensively, one should look for places whose food, supplemented by an endearing sordidness, a stylized squalor, transcends its own mediocrity. When it comes to food, we must cherish this: The exotic synthesis of antiquity and modernity, elegance and modesty, rather than the onanism of self-service chain stores and surgical cafeterias or the pandering of fancy restaurants.

In any city, there are countless restaurants that fall into the desirable category, which lies between extravagance and downright bad eating experiences. Here, then, are a few perhaps obscure examples whose food may resemble in its doubtful quality what we are accustomed to eating in the neighborhood but whose atmosphere proposes to save its kitchen from defamation. I do not pretend that these places offer incomparable eating experiences, but they do constitute a first step toward being one with your dinner and away from the perils of careless consumption.

Because abundant examples would only belabor a simple point, I cite eateries in just the Boston area with which I am familiar. Let's start with the Harvard Garden Grill on Harvard Square. In an area that caters to college crowds, the Garden Grill has miraculously not lost its innocence. The grill is substantial for three reasons: It has TV above the bar, a lot of cardboard placards to which are stapled things like Bromo, Cheez-Its, crackers and tins of sardines, and Hav-A-Hanks, and a lot of dark wooden booths. Small drafts are 15¢, and the sandwiches are disgraceful. One refreshing aspect is that there are never many students there. A juke box with Al Martino records stands in the corner. The old colonial white plaster ceiling is the same that can be found at Durgin Park, an eighteenth-century relic in which curtness and fair food pass for far better.

Two blocks from Durgin Park, on Haymarket Square, is Mondo's, a sober truck stop tucked inconspicuously between two blackened warehouses. It is relatively simple except for

its one charmingly vulgar extravagance; on the most prominent wall hangs an immense oil painting of a nude with
crimson lipstick, enormous entrées, and a torso elongated beyond the elasticity of the human anatomy. The obvious, but
affable errors in the painting speak well for Mondo's as a
restaurant.

Back in Cambridge, there is a spot that approaches the
interest of a cultural museum. The Varsity Spa stays open
only until three-thirty in the afternoon, but it is open from
near dawn until then. The window sills are caked with dust
and old boxes of Nabisco crackers; one wall of shelves is lined
with random canned goods from previous decades. The Coca-
Cola dispenser on the counter is a nostalgic relic—one of the
old red shiny rounded numbers which looks like a Packard's
back fender. The man and the wife who run it are friendly
beyond normal courtesy and will happily accommodate individual taste within the limitations of their menu. I like the
Varsity Spa the way some people like movies from the forties
featuring men in zoot suits and pointed shoes. Freaks and
derelicts are served; liquor and bratwurst are not.

In the North End, try the Cafe Sicilia which serves dime
pastry with green and orange frosting. Tony's, nearby, has no
menu. Tony just gets up in the morning and makes something. Tony's particular about boys' styles. If he doesn't like
it, he says he'll pin it up on the wall. That's not the only thing
Tony doesn't like. If you don't finish what he serves you, he
throws it at you. A little girl, maybe his daughter, comes
around with pictures of emaciated people who don't eat their
food. If you don't finish yours, she comes back, takes your
photo with an Instamatic, and then you get shown around.

If you're hungry in the middle of the night, pay a visit to
Kim Toy Lunch at Beach and Tyler in Chinatown. It's preferable to Dino's all-night pizza place a few blocks away because it has edible food. Kim Toy Lunch has a decent Won
Ton soup. The clientele is shady at late hours, mostly killers
and high school sharks, but the area is well protected.

Alfred Jarry, the French madman, once said that "If we must have murders, it's better that they should be works of art." It may be suspected from the preceding observations that I'm subscribing to a similar ethos by suggesting that if we must eat awful food, it should somehow be artfully awful and served in artfully decadent surroundings. To escape this charge gracefully, I must simply say that it's a start in learning to respect food and our own bodies to respect where we eat it. We forget that food comes mostly from the earth, from natural life, and that it should be eaten in natural places, restaurants true to themselves and true to their customers, not extracted from some entrepreneur's mind or plastiform mold.

Finally, we should learn to prepare food with the utmost care, finding that the biological and aesthetic aspects of food are actually inseparable. We don't eat food simply so that it can later leave our bodies; food is not something merely to insert in our systems. We must treat food as an art and not as a suppository. If we had respected it all along, we wouldn't be constipated in the first place.

Wherever You Go,
You End up in America:
Notes on a European Notebook

You had a bad year at school. America had become too much for you. You and your friends talked late into the night about radical politics, but your discussions went badly; they were the ruminations of a self-conscious tribe. When the summer came, you shrugged and went off to Europe.

You would have liked to begin your journal with a quote, but none occurred to you as you sat in your room in the Phoenix House on Argyle Street in London. It was the only single you could find, and it had no running water. But you took the room, which faced the street, the oily sidewalk, and the gargoyled church at King's Cross, and you took out your blank journal and you wrote: "I have taken a room in the Phoenix House on Argyle Street. It has no running water, but it was the only single I could find. It faces the street, the oily sidewalk, and the gargoyled church at King's Cross. I will have to do my washing in the tube lavatory."

At four o'clock, you bought a ten-cent pint of milk and took it to a balding park in the neighborhood. Birds, feeding on the lawn, suddenly arose and sped over your head, their red twigged legs pressed up against their bodies. A gaunt drunk soft-shoed to a slim audience. A woman cooed at pigeons through her gums. "I love children," the drunk warbled as his dancing lured a little girl from her family and her brother hastened after her, grabbing her by the hand and leading her back to the park bench. Apologetically, the whole family nodded and smiled at the dancer who quickly looked the other way and said, "I love children." An old lady with the sports section wrapped around her ankles snickered at him. He turned toward her and began to undulate to some concealed rhythm. Suddenly, he was jerking his bony pelvis at her, his body snapping inside his black pants. She pretended not to notice, but he continued to push in and out. The family got up from the bench and moved away. The pigeons scattered. Some other birds picked up and flew away, their dark choreography standing out against the sky. You let a few drops of the thick milk escape your mouth as you laughed. You were happy.

You had your first brown ale and glimpse of Scotch egg. You went to the London Zoo to see the penguins, and afterwards to the Wellington Pub where you drank with the proprietor of the Phoenix House, John More. You talked about America, his knowledge of which was broader, if not deeper, than yours, having seen much of it during his forty years at sea. You noticed his scalp condition, the crisp yellow flakes which encrusted his head.

After a Soho dinner (in your journal, you joked that it was "so-so"), you turned the corner in the syrupy orange streetlight. As you washed in the basin on the stand, you splashed water on the floor and it buckled the floor paper. Seeing the cabinet door at the foot of the bed unhinged, you decided to ignore everything. It was clear that the luxury of the room depended entirely on its negligence, on its careless grace.

Your thoughts, always tethered to your family and your darkening past, tore away. You had no idea who said "*Tous nos malheurs viennent de ne pas pouvoir être seul*," but you thought of that line. You walked over to the mirror, looked in your direction, and said, "I am alone." It didn't sound right.

Your life had not led directly, inexorably, to that condition, and you were not prepared for it. Instead of summer camp, your parents should have sent you off, at the age of nine or ten, to small dirty hotels in other cities to live by yourself for eight weeks. Instead of archery, canoeing, and handicrafts, you would instruct yourself in loitering, vagrancy, and begging. Instead of capture-the-flag on Saturday, you would sit in alien parks, crying your heart out for home. At the end of the summer, your parents would arrive in their station wagon to take you back in time for school.

Alone, you were still content, somehow even exultant. You thought of George Orwell down and out in London, and you felt warm inside. You finally realized you were not alone, not alone at all! You were simply in a situation that resembled loneliness. You would have been miserable were your friends and past to be kept from you forever, not just until your return to America. To have renounced your friends to an irretrievable tense would have killed even their recollection. But you knew that they were being preserved for you like TV dinners you could thaw out and enjoy later. When your grandfather fled Bucharest in 1914 on the eve of a war that would have destroyed him, he promised no one snapshots or little bronze miniatures of the Statue of Liberty on his return. He simply left, and he was alone.

For you, the solitude in the Phoenix House was instead like a tale you could tell everyone later; it was not a deprivation, but an occurrence. Not silence, just a lull. You were not alone; this whole adventure would make for some pretty interesting stories. You would tell them the next time you and your friends got together.

You talked to John in the Wellington about both world wars, which he was in, about Fifth Avenue in 1922, and tacos in San Pedro, California. After buying him another stout, you asked if you could have one of his cigarettes. You couldn't believe peoples' lives come to an end.

After dinner at the Maurina snack bar with friends, you paid the tiny bill. "That was terrible," you said as you walked out the door. "But it was the best meal I've had in a long time." The others agreed, and you all went off to see a feeble musical revue in Drury Lane.

To Portobello Road with a friend. Her fits of depression could be easily diagnosed as culture shock or just the difficulties of travel. You wrote in your journal: "There is nothing like a neurotic with transparent neuroses." Yet you respected her difficulties. You, on one hand, seemed so much at home in strange countries, gliding through strange cultures. She, on the other, was having the experience of being abroad. You saw the inability to find the correct bus as something easily overcome; she saw it as a small trauma. She became nervous and longed for home. Bored, you asked the conductor for the right bus. You never left home.

On the advice of a friend, you took the train to Chester on the way to Ireland, but you were disappointed when you arrived. You checked in at the YMCA, which was actually a mansion just outside the gates of the old city, and then explored the battlements, parapets, passageways; as it got late, the sun edged behind a turret. After showering, you walked again. It was dark. In the middle of a street you turned down in the old city, there was a crowd of young German or Austrian people, maybe your age, drinking on the sidewalk outside a pub, throwing their arms indiscriminately around each other. There were many pretty blond girls with thick, but pleasant, legs. You went inside, which was filled with young people, and ordered a lager which you carried back outside where you stood unobtrusively against a wall. Small groups talked with very animated gestures. When one of them appeared to turn to you, chattering, you quickly took a sip of your lager, which you hated. You didn't understand a word of their conversation. You shifted weight from one leg to another; you were the only person standing by yourself. You thought they were talking about you. Most of the boys wore blazers with an emblem on the pocket, indicating that they belonged to a youth society or tourist group. The girls belonged to them. Still, you fell in love with a dark-haired girl in a white dress. What could you say to her? You hoped that they would all leave before you could think of something to say. A boy jostled you as he went past, and you wanted to slug him. Finally, they all drifted away, yelling and pushing one another, and climbed into dark green buses with tinted windows. You had desired to know the girl in the white dress and had wanted to be asked to spend September with her in her father's Bavarian castle, or at least you had wanted to fist fight with her boyfriend, but you had, at the same time, carefully ensured that neither sort of thing would take place. As you walked back to the YMCA, you felt lonely again, but knew that it was the cheap kind of solitude. "With so much real loneliness around," you wrote, "why am I always stuck with this?"

In the train station the next day, you saw an American whom you had last seen three years ago in France. You had never known him in the States; your relationship consisted only of running into each other on your aimless excursions abroad. You were not sure if it was really he. He prowled the platform, sneaking glances at you which you circuitously returned. He pretended to read a magazine at the stand; you bought some candy, brushing against him at the counter. He paraded back and forth in front of you, talking pensively to his traveling companion. You looked him over when his back was turned. He removed a map from his knapsack and traced unfamiliar Welsh roads with his finger. Finally, you laughed loudly and said, "You're E. O., aren't you?"

"Yeah," he said, "and you're M. G., right?"

"Yeah! E. O., my god!"

"M. G., unbelievable!"

After the train ride to Holyhead, you and E. O. and his friend climbed up the street to an old Roman cemetery. You leaned against a wall and watched the night fall into the harbor below, among the cranes and ships and men drinking on the sidewalk in plaid slippers.

Then they took the ferry to Dublin, and you walked back to the green grocer's where you had been promised a room for the night. Then something happened: You were washing in the sink and a string of beads around your neck broke and the beads scattered all over the bathroom. You washed some down the drain and picked some up, and went into the bedroom. You turned off the light and looked out the window. Everything was completely black except for a lighted window across the way with a curtain. The darkness was supple, and you sank into it; you were afraid, but it was a soft fright. You forgot what floor your room was on and where in the city of Holyhead the green grocer lived. You could not have escaped if you had wanted to. You remembered the night you were staying at your cousin's pitch-black apartment in New York. At two in the morning, you were called out of your deep sleep by a long-distance phone call from a friend in another city. You could not imagine how he had found out where you were, so you assumed you were still in a dream which accepted any coincidence. The room was black. You talked without knowing what you were saying; you no longer knew on which side of consciousness you were. You hung up in the darkness and felt your way to the kitchen where you opened the refrigerator. You still did not know if you were dreaming or not. You actually pinched yourself, but you were still in the kitchen in the dark in front of the refrigerator. Looking in, you saw the bologna, the whipped cream, the ketchup, the sweet gherkins, and the club soda. And for an instant, a very short but intense instant, you thought you were dead. You thought, surely death begins with a long-distance phone call in the dark; now you were on the other side. Maybe, you thought, death is the instant which penetrates life, which doesn't negate it, but which shoots right through it to the other side, which exposes what is living to the desolation around it. Not the negation of the refrigerator, but this: To open the refrigerator in the dark kitchen at an hourless hour and to realize that that is all there is, you and the refrigerator. There is no one else, no dinner guests, not even hunger, just you and the refrigerator in the middle of the black and air-conditioned night. There is no moment before and no moment after, only the moment that contains you and the ice box and the soft blind banging of the dead into the kitchen walls.

Then you were moving toward Glencree, a town which has a graveyard built in memory of German fliers who lost their way and crashed in Ireland and a movie studio. You were hitchhiking, and the old man in an oversized coat who picked you up said, "I'm an extra in the movie here, but I only play in funeral scenes. That's because I have a face for funerals." Or were you hitchhiking from Casablanca to Tangiers, and there were gazelles on the deserts and Bedouins and a dusk and a sunset and flat land and when you got on the wood train at Marrakech, there were people clinging to the outside?

Or were you in Dublin, after a ferry ride, in a room in the O'Brien's home, a gray premeditated house in a suburb worse than any American development? You walked the repetitive blocks until you found a pub which was nothing more than another squat cement building called the Crescent Lounge or the Gay Dubliner. Later, you went to a fish 'n' chips place and consumed a discourteous piece of fried white fish. That night, you were sick to your stomach and dreamt of an immense piece of fried fish, glistening and brown, oozing fat, descending slowly overhead, finally blotting out the entire sky. You stayed in bed all day which was no better or worse than staying in bed in a suburb of Pittsburgh or Houston. In bed, you wrote in your journal:

I failed to claim for myself then any real emotion. I did not agonize over unrequited love or revel in requited love; I only agonized over the indistinctness of my feelings and only reveled in the independence I thought would protect me in the end. In the end, my independence has only landed me in the most irredeemable of situations, convalescing in an odorless suburb of Dublin. How absurd to jump from city to city, skimming the surfaces of Europe, as though one were leafing through a travelogue of pictures without captions.

You went to the Edinburgh Zoo this morning to see the penguins, despite the threat of rain.

You went to another city. A few weeks afterwards, you tried to recall its name, but couldn't even though it was a capital, or at least a very large city with heavy industry. You were put up at Mrs. K.'s apartment about ten minutes from the center of town. She was sixty-one and very warm and a widow. Her small apartment was like a museum; small Persian rugs overlapping on every floor, clumsy oil paintings on every wall; flowers, porcelain dolls and ashtrays, postcards, and momentos from southern vacations.

On a boat tour around the city, a professional photographer took your picture and then tried to sell you a print at the end of the ride. In the photo, you were sitting alone on one of the benches against the side of the boat, conspicuously separated from the others who were bunched together near the front. Your arm was poised on the edge and you were peering up strangely at the photographer as if reprimanding him for his intrusion. You did not buy a copy because, already, ten minutes after it was taken, it had become too bitterly nostalgic. You could see yourself in twenty years quietly explaining to guests that "This is me, at twenty, already a lonely traveler." And then someone would say, "Now, I bet you weren't as lonely as all that!"

Nostalgia was a wedge you drove between you and every experience.

You said good-bye to Mrs. K., but only after she showed you five hundred postcards from around the world and twenty-five party photos of her taken four years before. And each time she handed you a new picture of herself seated at the birthday table, she said in a surprised tone, as if the picture were supposed to be of someone else, "Ah! You see, that's me!"

In the large public garden, the sun was bright, taking up half the heavens. It was Sunday. There was no unnecessary noise or movement. Even the jet overhead was quiet and far away, as though it flew in another sky.

At some point, you fell in love. It happened in a city that was smaller than the last. On a Tuesday night, you and she were among five people on a sailboat, taking part in a race that began an hour before, at eight in the evening. No one seemed to know exactly where the crucial buoy was located, and boats were slicing in all directions. Clad in a bulky orange waterproof suit, you moved about stiffly. You were sitting on the bow and she was at the stern, pulling on a rope. It had rained heavily at the beginning of the race and the sky had turned a steely inimical blue. You looked over at her; she looked up at you. It was this moment, wasn't it, that you insisted on remembering. You smiled. A moment which had no potential; it had fulfilled itself. You chose it, among others, for yourself alone.

A year ago that day, your grandfather died. It was the day that it started, the day you started thinking of how bad leaving would be. You had begun to brood, and you were aware that she wasn't as she glided over events, accepting the relationship without sadness, as an irreversible moment of happiness. Through the living room window, you watched the ferry cross from one city to another. The odor of red cabbage came up to you from the kitchen. You were positive at that moment that life was proceeding irrevocably toward the future. The ferry, barring exceptional incident, would reach its destination in an hour and a half. You, barring exceptional incident, would be somewhere else in a few months, far away, remembering her with an odd and diffuse love. Knowing how imminent that future was, you longed for it then.

Her grandfather was senile and could not remember your name. After you had been introduced three times, you as-

sumed you were safely acquainted. But when you passed him
on the stairs, he stopped you and asked who you were. You
told him again. He said he was happy to meet you in fluent
English. When you were at the dinner table, he leaned over
and asked his daughter who you were. During the meal, he sat
opposite you in his tweed jacket and thick blue tie, his food
broken up in small pieces.

At the end of four days traveling in another country, you
were disturbed to see yourself in the big mirror of the guest
room in a small port where you were staying. You looked as
old as your father. Your whiskers were growing unmercifully
fast, spreading up your face and down your neck like an insidious forest of small black trees. On your chin, conditions
had become so crowded that the appearance of any more
whiskers would have required others to move elsewhere. That
was not all: Your whiskers were beginning to encroach upon
your features, showing no regard for your eyes, nose, or mouth.
You discovered a very prominent vein below your right eye,
greenish blue against the black shadow of your under-eye. You
were too young for this and studied yourself in the mirror.

You ate anchovies, bread, cheese, and soda in your room on
a piece of newspaper. You thanked God you could bring yourself to these solitudes and still go back to America in a few
weeks.

Other tourists hastened to the sites designated in their guide
books in the towns they visited; you rushed off to the department stores to cruise the aisles, to lose yourself in the colored
objects and notations of the culture. You felt terribly op-
pressed again, by boredom as well as loneliness, and as you
walked through a large store past deodorants, gloves, waxed
containers of Sunkist juice, and tins of Nivea, you began to
blink violently; it was a nervous habit of yours. You found
yourself walking past the same counter three times. It was
difficult for you to keep your eyes open, you were blinking so
hard. By the cosmetics, your eyes burned and you realized

that, for a long time, you had not been so close to powerful tears.

You eventually located yourself. You were in Paris, eating in a small Greek restaurant with three French friends. Alcohol, cigarettes, fatigue, the French language had all caught up with you, and suddenly your senses started to leave you. The others continued to eat. But you stared ahead, aware of the sounds receding, the lights diming, your hands and head becoming heavy, disembodied. You could not move; your vision was glassy and your shirt was soaked with sweat. A bemused observer of your own difficulties, you could communicate nothing to the others. French and English were equally useless to you. If I am dying, you thought to yourself, it's very pleasant. Although you were able to narrate the dissolution of your senses in your head, you were entirely outside of the event, with no wish to escape. As all your senses weakened, they merged, until you were aware only of the faint activity of life around you.

"*Qu'est-ce que tu as?*" a friend asked.

"*Mais je t'assure,*" you said, not even knowing you were speaking, "*ça ne fait rien.*"

Voices fell and rose around you. A waiter approached the table with a towel. Forms hovered expectantly above you. You had no desire, however, to utter clever last words.

"*Peut-être monsieur voudrait monter au WC?*"

You refused. Vomiting was out of the question. What you wanted to do was to wait patiently for the end. Across the table, your companions' faces became unfamiliar.

"*B'en, vas-y,*" someone exhorted you. "*Ça va mieux.*"

You were on the first step. Your legs were moving, but you were not responsible for them. You were on the second step. On the third, you tottered, blacked out. It was a standard faint, but not without its drama. Before you hit the stairs, three waiters gracefully arrived to catch you and carry you above their shoulders toward the street squeezing in between tables. You opened your eyes, but you were still overcome by a drunken synesthesia; dull lights and remote voices were indistinguishable. A sibilant wave curled over you. They put you down in a chair on the sidewalk. Your shirt was open, and wet. Young couples strolling by looked briefly at you over their shoulders. You nodded happily at them, pressing a cold cloth to your forehead.

The next day, you received a present of a Japanese kimono. You were content to be an American in a Japanese kimono drinking cider on a porch in a suburb of Paris.

You were lying in a meadow somewhere in the Swiss Alps. Perhaps it was the Pyrenees. Your verse was coming difficultly. Where your emotion fell short, you prodded your poems with false deliberation; you ascribed passion, in desperation, to your dullest thoughts. Words you would have liked to discard kept reappearing in the middle of lines. The sun was hot. The mountains were high. You didn't think you could write poems for a while, even though a boy down in the village had just died. His funeral was taking place in the square. The old men were all wearing dark shabby suits.

By traveling, you hoped to transcend your provincialism, to return bearing new languages and mannerisms as signs of worldliness. Yet your excursions only led back to your own illiberality. The farther you went into the hills above Montreux, the closer you got to your own Americanism. You never felt quite so much at home.

You only superimposed yourself on other countries; you got from them only those limited experiences you would receive from any situation. The scenery changed, but the scenario didn't. The trick would have been to forfeit all self-consciousness—to suffer a temporary amnesia, to have lost yourself in the foreign experience, not in the foreignness of the experience. But you isolated the unknown, that's all, and it became familiar.

You could not escape yourself psychically merely by changing geography. Being in France made you no less American; it made your cultural habits even more conspicuous by contrast. You realized how much you had written about death and loneliness, the things your political discussions in America had turned to after a while. You realized you carry the same luggage wherever you go.

In an effort to lose yourself in Europe, you concealed your prosperity, you imposed on yourself minor hardships. You slept on trains, traveled with a knapsack, became abstemious for no particular reason. You traveled three thousand miles in order to search for the solitude you could not locate in America. And even then, not to feel that. With a little originality, you could have uncovered genuine deprivations at home. You finally saw that this kind of austerity was the most ironic hedonism of all.

Traveling in Europe, you didn't discover yourself: You simply confirmed what you already were. Largely, your odyssey fulfilled a need your affluence created. Travel had become a nervous bourgeois habit. Wherever you go, you end up in America. And when you end up in America, you are never farther from home.

A Short Cultural History
of Salt Lake City

I found this poem in Salt Lake City on December 23, 1969.
It starts with a ride in the Chevy of a Boy who hates Niggers
and ends as Bronco Putnam, ex-cowboy Star who now works
with the navy YMCA in San Diego. I'll make it short because
we all have other things to do like the People in Salt Lake
City today who got no time for poems cause their Babies are
howling in the hungry wilderness of this nearsighted Far West
beyond which Art Teachers, Preverts, and Jane Fonda are
climbing up the other side and People here by the Utah Hotel shouldn't look at me like that just cause I don't wear Chaps
don't mean I have a gun in my pocket or my hand in your
Daughter's pine-scented private forest.

So the first thing I did after the Boy who won't come to
Chicago cause of the Niggers is I went to the Charles Discount Store which is owned by an older Jew who sold me two
pairs Socks and who had he found out I shared his God would
have probably sold me two pairs of two-toned saddle shoes and
talked my Heritage out of me. But I was off with my handsome Argyles to the Mormon Temple & Tabernacle & Visitor
Center wherein this statue of Adam & Eve Adam & Eve were
wearing robes while small fauna ran Unabashed in the ferns
of a salacious mural right behind them and I asked our guide

who had not, at the age of forty-three, yet befouled his body
with tobacco, alcohol, tea, or coffee, why I asked him do Adam
& Eve have clothes on. "That's just the way the artist did it,"
he stammered as though artists had the ability to sculpt fully
dressed Adams & Eves into our belief or draw Immaculate
Conceptions into the real world.

And after the movie *Man's Search for Happiness* in the
lower lobby in which Grandpa wades through a miasmic
heaven in a white shirt, white tie, and white Ducks to be
united with a tearful grandmother and a white Host of the
saved, I went to the Esquire Theater to cleanse myself and
see *Black Velvet*, a low-budget stag that cost maybe forty fifty
dollars in which Julie (Kim Alison) uses her behemoth body,
cleverly concealed throughout in layers of underwear and
oleo, to buy enough social mobility to climb from a truck-
stop waitress job to the high dive of the Las Vegas Starlie
where Brad her Boyfriend is shooting stills of her Ample
thighs and immense Copacabanas. And everyone in the
Theater was a sixty-four-year-old Man with jowls like pink
cumulus clouds, sitting by himself, including the Jew from
the Charles Discount Store whom I noticed across the aisle
who seemed not to be watching Joe clutching Julie's hard-
earned tips in the back of the Diner so much as wondering
How, in so few years, a Jewish family from Eastern Europe
could end up in Salt Lake City selling boots to families with
blinking Santas throbbing in their frontyards and babies bay-
ing for wisdom in their Western cribs.

And then I passed the John Birch Society Bookstore where
I read pamphlets and leaflets decrying the carnal, communist,
and concupiscible sins of this country and sex education and
Marx in the high schools and a Woman chewing Chiclets outside walking by looking in said Amen and shuffled down to
the corner. Later, eating at the Utah Cafe, I noticed a Man
sitting near me at the counter with no teeth and a beard and
a brown suit in which the pocket was filled with ball-point

pens lined up like Panatellas and of which the zipper was completely missing and he ate half his grilled cheese before putting the second Half, the chips, and carrot Curl into a brown paper sack and lighting a cigarette that was a Chesterfield and looking like Ezra Pound who was born not far from here in Hailey, Idaho. His name was Ed Osian, born in Salt Lake in 1895, educated at Andover and Yale before going to the war in 1917 after which he returned to the West to be with his lumber trade and sawmills and remembrances of Latin Poetry and New Haven and since his home burned down in town he lived flippantly in a flop House down the street with his Yale education and his small senilities while the people in the Utah Cafe had Daughters with piano teachers and thought he was queer cause he didn't shave and smoked the last acts of his cigarettes in a black holder.

And we traded addresses and I wanted to pay for his meal, but he said no and I left to catch a ride back to the snowy mountains South of the City and on the sidewalk I already had written him my first letter which went "Dear Ed, what are you doing in Salt Lake City, what are you doing in a narrow hotel, you who introduced Alpine skiing to the area and culture to the Utah Cafe; Why don't you at least go to Chicago where they have Niggers & Adams & Eves in the buff. Yours,"

The other passenger on my bus ride back to the mountains was Bronco Putnam who couldn't stop talking just as I'm sure he couldn't stop riding them dogies down years ago on TV and radio and when we passed a shiny blue pickup on South Temple Street, he said, "Jesus, what a pickup, I've never seen one like that before," and we stopped at a Colonel Sander's so he could get a chicken Snak and he came out and said, "Jee—sus, what a place, I've never seen a place like that before," and when the rain turned to snow halfway up the canyon, he said "Jee—sus, someone's shaking out a feather bed upstairs, don't you think?" and then he asked me where I went to school and when I got out he said, "Jesus, you were great to have along and whatever you are out of school, you're twice as good in it."

And Ladies & Gentlemen here the poem ends cause there's nothing comes after it except Bronco Putnam riding off in the sleeted night in the white bus to his Alpine Lodge and the Far Western stars twinkling America America up Above.

The Last Chapter

Making yet another wrong turn, I was suddenly navigating through an industrial plain in New Jersey. On one side, the horizon broken only by gaunt cranes and towers; on the other, a tidy New Jersey community swept upward to a crest, verging on New York. And there, soaring right out of a split level home sitting on the horizon, rising above its roof, an incomprehensible silver stalk, the top half of the Empire State Building, thrust right out of their living room. It seemed that the family who had waited years to escape the city and had finally secured a comfortable home across the river now found itself closer to the city than ever, the children required to play Scrabble in the shadow of one of the tallest buildings in the world. As for me, caught between Manhattan's density and New Jersey's useless, fetid spaces, caught between alternatives which defied choice, I panicked for a moment. But then, like one inured to enclosures, I calmed down, pacified by a condition that was, after all, so familiar.

I ran out of gas. Fuming, I coasted to a stop on the shoulder and stepped out on the edge of the poisoned tundra; in the heart of civilization, a thousand miles from it. I leaned against the car and watched the air thicken. Anger once again rose in me, then subsided. I smiled. I never felt safer. In fact, nothing would be more believable, predictable to me than to be left to die in Secaucus on the roadside as millions of vehicles raced by. In my head, I concocted the exact nature of my fate as a series of absorbing newspaper headlines.

After so long refusing to get inside experience, observing it from a distance, I discovered I had an almost Decadent affinity for the moment, this moment, the aesthetically perverse moment. So much could be said for even this intrusive, technological moment. But, in fact, I was just as detached as always. Frightened by the prospect of reckoning with the real, physical consequences of my position on the roadside, I willed myself to participate in the moment artistically. It was, as always, the coerced literary moment of attention to detail, and nothing else. The horrifying instant of claustrophobic danger was turned neatly into a moment of artistic, sardonic humor.

Is it by some mistake that we find ourselves safely back in our homes, in our friends' apartments, the door skillfully locked behind us? Is it through some special magic that we can go shopping and return unharmed? I am surprised that the violent intricacy of the world has, until now, excluded me from its plots. A cop in a squad car stops at a red light on the North Side. He waits. A sniper on the twentieth floor of a housing project blows his head off. Assuming his motor has stalled, the other cars carefully wind their way around him when the light changes. I am surprised that I have been ignored by these men with impeccable aim. There was a short period of time recently when, newly impressed with my vulnerability, I would flinch as I passed cars while driving down darkened streets. I jerked my head forward at the instant I expected to be shot, deftly evading the bullet. A dance is held just outside of Grenoble. To insure its exclusiveness, all exits but one are pad-locked and boarded. There is a fire. Only twenty people escape; the other 145, all in their teens and early twenties, are burned to death. People in passing cars stop, but don't understand. Refusing to believe what they are told, refusing to help, they choose to laugh.

I have always been among those twenty. Taking this good fortune for granted sometimes, I begin to believe that somehow I am entitled to eternal safety from these dangers. What happens around me is so casually cataclysmic that I expect either to be destroyed or, managing to escape, find perpetual freedom. Apocalypse would content me, as a vindication of my fears. To live my life untouched, at some exquisite spiritual pitch, would also content me, of course, as a vindication of my fondest hopes. I imagine one or the other, but nothing in between, not that zone of life in which one must contend with the threats, but not the easy consummation, of the end.

We are members of a telescopic age whose moments slip quietly into one another and are seldom heard from again. Incidents pile up in a simultaneous heap. The first and last moments touch; birth and death are juxtaposed at My Lai. Our priorities are disturbed; accessible details take precedence over unapproachable catastrophes. Although the electronic information age informs us of activities in the most obscure corners of the world, we can no longer remember how many wars there are; current events serve only to remind us of our frailty. And those who could really tell us what it is like, those people murdered at Orangeburg, Jackson State, Kent State, and Phnom Penh, simply are not around anymore to astonish us with their statistics.

Even our sentiments, compressed into frenetic states of mind, are unintelligible. Do our ills belong to us or to the history we are living through? We have become as impatient as events. We are tempted to ask that moral and emotional progress be as rapid as technological change. Because we speak to someone on the other coast, dialing direct, we can't believe our love will go wrong. Now that families use electric knives in their kitchens, we can't believe that they still vote for the wrong candidates. When we watch a football game in a stadium with sixty thousand people, we can't understand that we are still alone.

Sitting up in this loft in the largest city in America. Outside, a truck passes. Or shall we say it was a cab? I had capuccino in a cafe; make it War Shu duck at Sam Wo. A chocolate egg cream at the corner. Rib roast at your son-in-law's. Really, how can we choose? A woman passes below the window, vericose, a transient in her own home. There is a suggestion about her that the choices she has made have not always been the correct ones, but they have been choices nonetheless, choices which have left her on the Lower East Side, living out her handsome life in a country that has been handed over to others. As far as choices are concerned, one might even say that she has played it safe. She could be eighty; to her, the years must be like faces in a crowd. To me, though, the years are distinct, each one with different features. One has a nose that is too large, another has eyes which are narrow, querulous. To her, the years are now just a wash of inaccurate flesh; but in each face I can see the pores.

Suppose that I really will dwell on the earth, that I will neither fall dead on the New Jersey Turnpike nor find everlasting happiness somewhere else, but that I will dwell with all the others in that graceless region in between, taunted by possibilities clearly beyond my reach and harrowed by disasters that will spare me? I see that all these pages have been written on that precipice, notes deposited on the edge of a tenuous future.

As I get closer to the beginning of this book, there is always the question of how the story ends. The problem of all those possible images, each one concealing a different and complicated fate: my seventy year old cousin, for instance; educated and talented, he was simply unwilling to put up with the idiotic demands of the world of his relatives. He excused himself. He now lives pennilessly in a black neighborhood on the

West Side of Chicago, although it is rumored that he is saving a modest inheritance for cousins who have even less than he. He is in the habit of showing up unexpectedly at family affairs, picnics, and funerals, draped in a variety of old coats, carrying a sandwich wrapped in tin foil. Except for these guest appearances, he lives apart, a form circulating on the periphery of our interests. I will not forget the sight of him in a fashionable living room, his pants rolled up to mid-calf, demonstrating to his immaculate audience an astounding array of rope tricks.

I had never truly considered that sort of thing for myself. A life in which each moment rebels against the previous one, a life predicated on resistance, once seemed reserved only for those insistent pariahs who failed to pursue more orthodox careers and lived in apartments without the benefit of TV and Listerine. Now that we are all desperados, every hideaway is tender with threats. I have imagined a life at the foot of a mountain. I have even seen myself as a taxidermist, spending my last days in the shadows of an Arizona office, stroking the heads of my quiet birds.